Advance Praise for *Authentic Leadership*

"All people who aspire to lead a company should read this book. It describes what a leader must do and be. It is not an easy course, but one that ultimately is very satisfying. Bill George led the company so clearly and openly with the use of the Mission. This man is an example of one of the world's greatest leaders. Learn from him."

—Earl E. Bakken, founder and director emeritus, Medtronic, Inc.

"Values. Stewardship. Authenticity. Compassion. Soul. Self-discipline. Yes, such words can still be applied to business leadership. And Bill George, who has walked the integrity walk in every step of his distinguished career, has earned the right to use them. This marvelous book will restore your faith in capitalism's potential for good."

—John C. Bogle, founder and former CEO, The Vanguard Group

"At a time when character-based leadership is in high demand and short supply, Bill George shows the way. *Authentic Leadership* should be required reading for new MBA's—and those who hire them."

—Richard E. Cavanaugh, president and CEO, The Conference Board

"This book is an extraordinary summary of what one of the finest executives of our time has learned about how to lead a company. Every aspiring leader needs to learn from Bill George's perspective, humility, and example."

—Clayton Christensen, author, *The Innovator's Dilemma*

"*Authentic Leadership* is a book that is especially pertinent for developing leaders. It sparkles with the experience, wisdom, and great stories of a trustworthy mentor."

—Max De Pree, former chairman and CEO, Herman Miller, Inc.

"*Authentic Leadership* reminds us that enduring principles are such because they are real and true. It's a must-read for today's aspiring business leaders. Through this book and through his personal example, Bill George shows us that over the long haul 'good guys' can and do win."

—Roger Enrico, retired chairman and CEO, PepsiCo

"The blend of wisdom, thoughtfulness, and personal reflection of Bill George's *Authentic Leadership* is quite unique. I hope that the book is widely read. It certainly deserves to be."

—Jeffrey Garten, dean, Yale School of Management, and
  author, *The Mind of the CEO*

"Bill George has won a legendary reputation for success and integrity in American enterprise, and now, at last, he has captured his story on paper. Here, in a book written from the heart, he shows how others can become what he is: a model CEO, family man, and human being. Read and grow!"

—David Gergen, director, Center for Public Leadership,
  Harvard University

"In a time when ethical leadership has more value than ever, Bill George shows us the way with clarity and conviction. He speaks with quiet authority, having lived this compelling important message. *Authentic Leadership* is both sound and inspiring, a valuable guide for any leader."

—Daniel Goleman, coauthor, *Primal Leadership*

"Bill George has written a penetrating and uniquely insightful book. With his emphasis on authentic leadership and a customer-focused business model, he has created an invaluable guide for today's CEOs and those who aspire to build innovative, mission-oriented companies."

—Dick Grasso, chairman and CEO, New York Stock Exchange

"At a time when confidence in corporate leaders is near its all-time low, Bill George makes a compelling case that we need a new generation of leaders to take charge—leaders committed to their purpose and values who know how to build enduring organizations that succeed for the long-term. His message is both timeless and vital."

—Rajat Kumar Gupta, managing director, McKinsey & Company

"Most business insiders know Bill George as the CEO's CEO—the real deal. A man who did it all: raising Medtronic's shareholders' value sixty-fold while fulfilling the firm's mission. In an era of shattered business idols, George illustrates how his fundamental values—integrity, spirituality, passion, candor, and tough-mindedness—shaped the authentic leadership that helped to create these results. He tells his story beguilingly, in the form of business stories that read like biblical parables in their moral acuity and compelling narrative."

—Regina Herzlinger, author, *Customer-Driven Health Care*

"Bill George's new book, *Authentic Leadership,* is full of insights to inspire new and current leaders. I highly recommend it."

—(Rev.) Theodore M. Hesburgh, C.S.C., president emeritus,
University of Notre Dame

"*Authentic Leadership* provides an excellent framework for twenty-first century leadership. Companies of the future must be both great and good. They must compete harder than ever in a brutal global market-place . . . while creating an environment that is focused on customers, respects individual employees, and builds trust with investors. *Authentic Leadership* describes ways that leaders must change to stay contemporary. I had a wonderful opportunity to learn from Bill George in several business ventures. Here Bill gives a broader audience a chance to benefit from his wisdom."

—Jeffrey Immelt, chairman and CEO, General Electric

"Few CEOs have as much credibility as Bill George when it comes to defining the ingredients for lasting success. He grew Medtronic into one of the world's most admired, values-driven enterprises. Now through his perception and useful new book, smart managers everywhere can learn from Bill George's broad experience and wisdom about what really matters."

—Rosabeth Moss Kanter, author, *The Change Masters*
and *When Giants Learn to Dance*

"Bill George is one of the most successful business leaders of all time. In this book, he describes what real leadership is. It is about people, integrity, character, values, empowerment, passion, compassion, stakeholders, teamwork, and purpose beyond self. This book is a must-read for today's leaders and for those who aspire to be leaders."

—Richard M. Kovacevich, chairman and CEO, Wells Fargo and Co.

"Anyone interested in how to become an effective leader should meet Bill George, former CEO of one of America's finest companies—Medtronic. The next best way to improve your leadership skills is to read Bill's extra-ordinarily readable and compelling book, *Authentic Leadership.* It's a virtual handbook of easy-to-follow leadership ideas."

—Arthur Levitt, former chairman, U.S. Securities
and Exchange Commission

"Bill George is an authentic leader. In *Authentic Leadership* he shares the guiding principles that he has adhered to with such great success. It is must-reading for CEOs and those hoping to become CEOs. It will be an outstanding textbook for a business school course in leadership."

   —Martin Lipton, managing partner, Wachell, Lipton, Rosen & Katz

"Bill George has written a very important and timely book. Based on his immense insight and experience, he gives us a convincing view of how leadership can shape the corporation of the future. Excellence through enlightened leadership is what this book is all about."

   —Peter Lorange, president, International Institute
     of Management Development (IMD)

"*Authentic Leadership* provides a critically important message about the type of leadership it will take to restore confidence in corporate America. Bill George has written a book filled with important ideas based on his successful tenure as CEO and board chairman of Medtronic and board member of some of the world's great companies. Unlike the spate of ego-driven memoirs by chief executives, Bill George's book gives us not only substance but that rarest of qualities—wisdom. *Authentic Leadership* should be required reading for all current and aspiring business leaders!"

   —Jay Lorsch, professor, Harvard Business School,
     and author, *Aligning the Stars*

"*Authentic Leadership* is candid, provocative, and a compelling call to action. It is a priceless dialogue with Bill George, unquestionably America's pre-eminent steward of corporate integrity. He walks the talk, leads from the heart, and never stops challenging business leaders to Get Real on honesty, responsibility, and purpose. This book is destined to be a classic."

   —Harvey Mackay, author, *Swim with the Sharks Without Being Eaten Alive*

In *Authentic Leadership*, Bill George shows why he is recognized as one of the world's best corporate leaders. He cuts straight to the core of building the effective organization—the ability of leaders to see problems, speak about them honestly, and provide the inspiration and passion to move forward. This is a must-read for those who believe, as I do, that every member of an organization can find a way to lead.

   —Hank McKinnell, chairman and CEO, Pfizer

"*Authentic Leadership* is a powerful call for genuine and ethical business leadership, made ever more persuasive by Bill George's own extraordinary life. His book preaches what Bill George has practiced over his long and incredibly successful career."

   —Walter Mondale, former vice president of the United States

"*Authentic Leadership* gives everyone who reads it a rare gift—the opportunity to be mentored by a brilliant yet caring man. Bill George gives us courage to live and lead with purpose, discipline, and heart. It couldn't come at a better time."

   —Marilyn Carlson Nelson, chairman and CEO, Carlson Companies

"Bill George is to the transformation of corporate leadership what Gandhi was to the transformation of political leadership: a visionary example that values-based, authentic leadership is powerful, effective, and profitable. *Authentic Leadership* can help restore both corporate values and value."

   —Dean Ornish, M.D., author, *Dr. Dean Ornish's Program for Reversing Heart Disease*

"For thirty years, Bill George has been a true leader: courageous, purposeful, and genuinely authentic. His message—that companies can create goods but must also create good—is important for everyone doing business today. I along with other business leaders will always be able to rely on this book as a standard reference."

   —Henry Paulson, chairman and CEO, Goldman Sachs

"*Authentic Leadership* offers new hope to anyone who has come to doubt the foundations of capitalism and the integrity of its true leaders. With the credibility of an insider, Bill George reminds us that corporate sustainability is based on values, not share value, and building a great corporation is not too different from building a great life. A must-read for anyone who dreams of a fuller life, both personally and professionally."

   —Rachel Naomi Remen, M.D., author, *Kitchen Table Wisdom*

"George's important new book is a refreshing look inside the executive suite. He courageously shares his hopes and humility, his dreams and disappointments, his triumphs and tragedies. Through uncommon personal revelations, this book goes far deeper than the many self-congratulatory CEO books. George transcends mythical tough-muscled leadership to look uniquely at the genuine importance of wisdom, credibility, and humanity. *Authentic Leadership* provides emerging leaders with the wisdom that truly effective leadership styles are shaped by one's values, experience, and choices. Leaders of any age will be inspired by this book to trigger life-changing self-examination."

> —Jeff Sonnenfeld, associate dean, Yale School of Management, and author, *The Hero's Farewell*

"Bill George was a leader in corporate governance before corporate governance was cool. Bill George has walked the governance walk, so he is one of the few whose governance talk is a must-read for anyone interested in optimal corporate performance."

> —Sarah Teslik, president, Council of Institutional Investors

"Bill George's book is a timely road map for twenty-first century leaders who realize that what's best for their customers, employees, shareholders, and communities is also what's best for long-term business success."

> —Bob Ulrich, chairman and CEO, Target Corporation

"Mission, integrity, and inspiration: A chief executive graphically explains how he led his company through extraordinary times, and how we might achieve the same if we build on the best within us. Bill George's *Authentic Leadership* is *the* primer for a new generation of managers who would look beyond the bottom line to engage, to serve, to lead. The final pages about his final day in the office is worth the price of admission alone."

> —Michael Useem, professor, Wharton Business School, and author, *The Leadership Moment*

"In *Authentic Leadership*, Bill George shares with great candor his beliefs and experiences as a successful leader and businessman. His work calls for a new generation of leaders, who are less concerned by appearance and conformity than by purpose and values. He illustrates with conviction and clarity that only by knowing oneself and being authentic can one achieve true leadership and sustainable performance."

> —Daniel Vasella, M.D., chairman and CEO, Novartis

"This is the best book by a business leader that I've ever read! It provides a wonderfully inspiring road map for what makes a great business. It's a must-read for every aspiring leader in any field."

> —John C. Whitehead, former chairman and CEO, Goldman Sachs

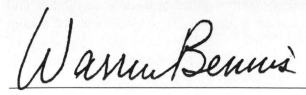

A WARREN BENNIS BOOK

This collection of books is devoted exclusively to new
and exemplary contributions to management thought
and practice. The books in this series are addressed to
thoughtful leaders, executives, and managers of all
organizations who are struggling with and committed
to responsible change. My hope and goal is to spark
new intellectual capital by sharing ideas positioned at
an angle to conventional thought—in short, to publish
books that disturb the present in the service of a
better future.

Books in the Warren Bennis Signature Series

Authentic Leadership

Bill George

Foreword by Warren Bennis

Authentic Leadership

Rediscovering the Secrets to Creating Lasting Value

JOSSEY-BASS
A Wiley Imprint
www.josseybass.com

Published by Jossey-Bass
A Wiley Imprint
989 Market Street, San Francisco, CA 94103-1741   www.josseybass.com

Jossey-Bass books and products are available through most bookstores. To contact Jossey-Bass directly call our Customer Care Department within the U.S. at 800-956-7739, outside the U.S. at 317-572-3986 or fax 317-572-4002.

Jossey-Bass also publishes its books in a variety of electronic formats. Some content that appears in print may not be available in electronic books.

Credits are on page 218.

Library of Congress Cataloging-in-Publication Data

George, Bill (William W.)
  Authentic leadership : rediscovering the secrets to creating lasting value / Bill George ; foreword by Warren Bennis.—1st ed.
      p. cm.
"A Warren Bennis book."
Includes bibliographical references and index.
  ISBN 0-7879-6913-3 (alk. paper)
  1. Leadership. 2. Organizational effectiveness. I. Title.
  HD57.7.G458 2003
  658.4'092—dc21

                                                    2003005592

Printed in the United States of America
FIRST EDITION
HB Printing   10 9 8 7 6 5 4 3 2

Contents

Foreword

"We need authentic leaders, people of the highest integrity, committed to building enduring organizations. We need leaders who have a deep sense of purpose and are true to their core values. We need leaders with the courage to build their companies to meet the needs of all their stakeholders, and who recognize the importance of their service to society."

These are the opening words to Bill George's remarkable book, *Authentic Leadership*, a book I'm so proud to have in this series because it speaks to the need and challenges for the leaders of tomorrow, our trustees of the future. The recent corporate scandals and crimes have had a devastating effect not only on the stock market but more importantly on the honorable profession of management. So pervasive was the cloud over American business that Intel's Andy Grove declared, "These days I'm ashamed I'm part of corporate America." Bill George's book, which is at bottom a Declaration of the Spirit and Values of Leadership, will most certainly restore a sense of honor to the noble calling of leadership, not just for business leaders but for leaders of all organizations: not-for-profits, NGOs, educational, and—I needn't remind anyone—for church leaders as well.

This book looks deeply and critically at vital questions such as, What are the purposes of the corporation and other organizations in today's world? The metaphor of the organization as a machine that creates values for shareholders is too simplistic, everyone agrees. But what metaphors are more illuminating? Bill George makes a case for viewing a company or other organizations as a *community* in a world where we spend more and more of our lives in the workplace and grow ever hungrier for greater balance between work and personal life. Even as we are shackled by our pagers and cell phones to the workplace, we long for work that seems meaningful enough to justify missing out on great chunks of our children's lives. Leaders of every kind of organization need to be thinking long and hard about such issues as meaningful rewards for workers and humanizing the downsized workplace. It would be tragic if the recent scandals so distracted and preoccupied leaders that they failed to address these more philosophical concerns. And it would be even more tragic if the scandals were to cause business to be perceived as an unworthy calling, just as political scandals have so often tainted public service in the past. This book goes a long way to restoring confidence, not only with those leaders who are exemplary moral and ethical and spiritual role models but also to those who are aspiring leaders.

Timeless leadership is always about character, and it is always about authenticity. Let me underscore the observation made by the pioneering psychologist, William James, about authenticity. "I have often thought," he wrote, "that the best way to define a man's character is to seek out the particular mental or moral attitude in which, when it came upon him, he felt himself most deeply and intensively active and alive. At such moments, there is a voice inside which speaks and says, 'This is the real me.'" This book will urge you to discover and cultivate that authentic self, the part of you that is most alive, the part that is most you.

Personally, I want to thank Bill George for this book. In my view it is one of the most honest and, yes, authentic books by a business leader I've ever read. While I was editing this book, I was reminded of the Roman emperor Aurelius, who was an OK leader but will be remembered more for his *Meditations* than his leadership qualities. Bill George will be remembered as much, perhaps more, for this book as for his extraordinary leadership achievements over the last four decades.

May 2003   WARREN BENNIS
Santa Monica, California

Preface

A New Generation of Leaders

Authentic: genuine; worthy of trust, reliance,
or belief

This book is written for the new generation of leaders—from recently elected CEOs to students considering whether they want to become leaders, and all the leaders in between who are preparing for added responsibilities. Its message is simple to state but challenging to realize: we need *authentic leaders* to run our organizations, leaders committed to stewardship of their assets and to making a difference in the lives of the people they serve.

Raised in the era of President John F. Kennedy and the New Frontier, my generation started out idealistically confident that we could change the world through our leadership. Along the way many leaders were seduced by immediate opportunities for personal wealth and wound up sacrificing the future of their organizations and the people they led.

Having been a corporate executive for more than thirty years, the last ten as CEO of Medtronic, I have known a vast array of business leaders and the companies they work for. All my experiences lead me to the same conclusion: when leaders are dedicated stewards and lead in an authentic manner, they build enduring organizations that do great good for people and make an enormous difference in the world. Are we prepared to permit greed to distract us from this goal and lead us down a path of destruction?

I wrote this book to convince current and future leaders that *there is a better way* to lead companies—a way that builds strong, enduring organizations and benefits all a company's stakeholders, its customers, employees, and shareholders. It doesn't mean authentic leaders won't be rewarded for their efforts. In fact, their rewards will reach far beyond well-earned monetary rewards to the satisfaction of making a difference in the lives of customers, providing great opportunities for employees, and generating superior long-term returns for shareholders. At the same time, authentic leaders lead authentic lives and have time to share with their families.

The book also examines the relationship between leaders and the organizations they lead. It shows how leaders grow from the interaction with their organizations in creating authentic companies. It demonstrates that their organizations are highly effective in competing in the market.

Writing this book has been a source of great joy, affording as it did the challenge of condensing all my leadership philosophies into a single, logical narrative. While I didn't set out to write an autobiography, it was only natural to use personal experiences in describing the challenges authentic leaders face and how they can be dealt with. Throughout the book I have endeavored to be candid, open, and introspective.

The Introduction offers a perspective on how the current leadership crisis developed and the proposition that the solution requires new leadership, not new laws. Part One describes the dimensions of authentic leaders, illustrates how leaders develop through transformational experiences, and examines leading an authentic life by balancing work and home life.

Part Two explores how leaders build authentic companies. It presents the central proposition that mission-driven companies create far greater shareholder value over the long term than do financially oriented companies. It shows how values-centered organizations become peak performers, and how companies that empower their employees generate superior customer service. It makes the case that it is great teams, not charismatic CEOs, that build great organizations. The last chapter shows how authentic companies generate superior results for all their stakeholders.

Part Three shows how authentic companies compete in the marketplace, looking first at the seven pitfalls that break the growth cycle of successful companies. The succeeding chapters explore what companies must do to fulfill their missions, look at ethical dilemmas and how they are resolved, and probe the process leading to breakthrough innovations. The concluding chapters propose that acquisitions should not be primarily about money but to build organizations, and address the challenges of meeting the needs of various stakeholder groups.

Part Four goes beyond the bottom line to look at the crucial differences between governing and managing, when it is time for leaders to take their case to the public arena, and how to prepare for succession and move on to new challenges. The Epilogue issues a challenge to future leaders to make a meaningful difference in the world.

My deepest hope is that these ideas will help inspire a new generation of leaders to lead authentically and build authentic companies.

May 2003   BILL GEORGE
Minneapolis, Minnesota

*This book is dedicated to
the most important person in my life, my wife, Penny,
whose love and counsel enabled me to develop into a
successful leader.*

Authentic Leadership

Introduction

Where Have All the Leaders Gone?

Thank you, Enron and Arthur Andersen.

The depth of your misconduct shocked the world and awakened us to the reality that the business world was on the wrong track, worshiping the wrong idols, and headed for self-destruction. Like the proverbial frog that dies when temperatures are gradually increased but immediately jumps out when tossed into a boiling pot of water, we needed this kind of shock therapy to realize that something is sorely missing in many of our corporations. What's missing? In a word, leadership. *Authentic leadership*.

What began as a few executives charged with violating the law morphed into issues of corporate governance and the failure of our governance systems. As we begin to understand these same issues at a deeper level, we realize that the missing ingredients in corporations are leaders committed to building authentic organizations for the long term.

Every generation has corporate thieves who break the law to reward themselves. This time around the excesses are not limited to a few. I believe deeply that the vast majority of corporate CEOs are honest leaders dedicated to building their companies. Unfortunately, far too many leaders got caught up by the short-term pressures of the stock market and the opportunities it brought for personal wealth. Under these pressures and enmeshed in the quest for personal gain, they wound up sacrificing their values and their stakeholders.

Our system of capitalism is built on trust—trust that corporate leaders and boards of directors will be good stewards of their resources, providing investors with a fair return. There can be no doubt that many leaders have violated that trust. As a result, investors lost confidence and withdrew from the market. In the process, many people got hurt, not just the perpetrators.

A *Time*/CNN poll taken in the summer of 2002 reported that 71 percent of those polled feel that "the typical CEO is less honest and ethical than the average person." In rating the moral and ethical standards of CEOs of major corporations, 72 percent rated them "fair" or "poor." A similar survey by the *Wall Street Journal Europe* reported that only 21 percent of European investors believe that corporate leaders are honest.

In the midst of the current crisis, we must ask ourselves, *where have all the leaders gone?* Where are today's versions of James Burke of Johnson & Johnson, Walter Wriston of Citicorp, John Whitehead of Goldman Sachs, and David Packard of Hewlett-Packard? These people not only built great enterprises but were statesmen in the business community and leaders in addressing societal issues as well.

In contrast, most leaders of today's best-run corporations remain silent. Are they afraid that by speaking out they may invite scrutiny of their companies? In so doing, they give the impression that they have something to hide or are also part of the problem. Only a few CEOs, such as Henry Paulson of Goldman Sachs and Henry McKinnell of Pfizer, have been willing to condemn these practices publicly, recognizing the larger issue is one of public trust in the capitalist system. Paulson's acts were doubly courageous, as he risked not only criticism from his peers but his customers as well.

Andy Grove, chairman of Intel, commented recently, "I find myself embarrassed and ashamed to be a businessman." These sentiments were echoed by a rising star at Medtronic, the medical technology company I led for a dozen years. He told me how angry he was at the executives who had damaged the reputations of all business leaders, saying he was reluctant to tell friends that he too is a corporate executive.

Capitalism Becomes the Victim of Its Own Success

How did we get in this situation? Is this a recent phenomenon, or have these activities been going on all along?

We are witnessing the excesses of the shareholder revolution that began fifteen years ago. In its early stages, pressure from shareholders did much to improve the competitiveness of American corporations, as companies trimmed unnecessary expenses, improved profitability, and increased cash flow. However, the financial rewards from their actions, both corporate and personal, were so great that companies and shareholders alike developed an inordinate focus on short-run results. In a booming stock market, it all seemed to be working.

Then capitalism became the victim of its own success. Instead of traditional measures such as growth, cash flow, and return on investment, the criterion for success became meeting the expectations of the security analysts. Investments were cut back to reach earnings targets, limiting the company's growth potential. Driven by speculators and security analysts, expectations kept rising, just as companies were struggling to make their numbers. Companies that met or exceeded the "magic" earnings number were handsomely rewarded with ever-rising stock prices. Those that fell short, even if they recorded substantial increases, were inordinately punished, and shareholders demanded replacement of the CEO. No wonder many CEOs went to extreme measures to satisfy shareholders!

However, revenues and earnings do not escalate forever, especially in the face of economic downturns, events like September 11, and operating problems. To offset financial problems, many executives stretched the numbers and the accounting rules well beyond their intended limits. Some of these accounting schemes, like calling operating expenses "capital equipment" to avoid the P&L and booking revenues before they were earned, violated even the most basic rules of accounting. Now the chickens are coming home to roost.

In the past five years stock options went from modest perks to mega-grants for top executives, especially CEOs. Because options had no cash impact and were not charged against profits, many executives and boards viewed these grants as free. The effect was to shift CEOs' focus almost entirely to getting the stock price up—by whatever means necessary. Realizing they could not sustain their earnings, many CEOs cashed in their options for huge gains just before their stock collapsed.

The general public played a role in this tragedy as well. In idealizing the high-profile personalities that ran these companies, we made them into heroes. We equated wealth with success and image with leadership. To our dismay, we have learned that these celebrity CEOs have been filling up their personal coffers at their shareholders' expense, while destroying the pensions and life savings of thousands of people.

The media turned these short-term earnings artists into the folk heroes of the business community. While making wealth, image, and star power the criteria for success, the media overlooked the many solid corporate leaders building quality companies for the long term. Ken Lay, Bernie Ebbers, and Dennis Koslowski were the focus of intense media worship before their fall. Just one year before he was led off to jail in handcuffs, *Business Week* named Koslowski "CEO of the Year" for being first on its Nifty Fifty list of top stock performers. These three executives alone have destroyed over $300 billion in shareholder value.

Back in 1998 I met with one of these leaders to talk about acquiring one of his companies. In our brief meeting he explained how his offshore headquarters enabled his company to avoid U.S. taxes, how he automatically issued pink slips to 25 percent of the workers on the day he acquired their company, and how he shut down every research project or investment that didn't pay off in the first year. As I walked out of his office, I held onto my wallet and decided to cancel further talks with him. You cannot do business with people you do not trust.

The Case for New Leadership

In response to the violations, policymakers and politicians have crafted new laws and regulations to close the loopholes. But although some changes in regulations are appropriate and necessary, they do not address the deeper issues at stake here. It is impossible to legislate integrity, stewardship, and sound governance.

Somewhere along the way we lost sight of the imperative of selecting leaders that create healthy corporations for the long term. The lessons of building great companies like 3M, Coca-Cola, Johnson & Johnson, General Electric, Pfizer, and Procter & Gamble were lost in the rush to get the stock price up. We forgot that those of us who are fortunate enough to lead great companies are the stewards of legacies we inherited from past leaders and the servants of our stakeholders.

The lessons from this crisis are evident: if we select people principally for their charisma and their ability to drive up stock prices in the short term instead of their character, and we shower them with inordinate rewards, why should we be surprised when they turn out to lack integrity?

We do not need executives running corporations into the ground in search of personal gain. We do not need celebrities to lead our companies. We do not need more laws.

We need new leadership.

We need authentic leaders, people of the highest integrity, committed to building enduring organizations. We need leaders who have a deep sense of purpose and are true to their core values. We need leaders who have the courage to build their companies to meet the needs of all their stakeholders, and who recognize the importance of their service to society.

If you yearn for authentic, moral, and character-based leaders, read on. If you aspire to be an authentic leader, this book is written for you. My objective is to offer a fresh approach to the business leaders of tomorrow, refined in the crucible of real-world experience. I believe it is an approach that not only will produce better leaders for our organizations but also will ensure the long-term viability and success of their companies.

Challenges Confronting Emerging Leaders

In recent years, I have gotten to know many rising leaders. Almost without exception, they have solid values and a sense of purpose. They are looking for something different in their lifetimes—the opportunity to contribute to a worthwhile cause through their work, to make a difference in the world, to find a reasonable balance between their work and home lives, and, most of all, to work for a company where they trust the leaders and share a similar set of values.

In my discussions with them, I hear a common set of questions:

- What's the purpose of my leadership? Do I really want to devote my talents to business?
- How can I find a job where I can make a real difference?
- Do I have to check my values at the office door?
- Is it possible to have a meaningful career and a successful family life? Is it worth it to work so hard?
- How can I stay true to my values when there are so many pressures to compromise?
- How do I balance the conflicting needs of my customers and my employees with the requirement to make the bottom-line numbers?
- Can I develop close relationships with my subordinates and still achieve my objectives?
- Do I have a responsibility to our society, for the environment, for global sustainability, for the gap between rich and poor? What can I do?

There are no easy answers to these questions, yet that shouldn't keep us from talking about them. These are precisely the questions that I have wrestled with throughout my life, as have so many of my peers. The real difference between my generation and the next is that the aspiring leaders of today are demanding answers to these questions *before* they commit to a company and a career path. To that I say, "Bravo!"

Unlike the many books on leadership written by observers of leaders, this one is written by someone who has spent his entire life on the playing field, learning how to lead and working to become a better leader. My purpose is *not* to hold myself up as a model of virtue or success. Rather, I want to share how I dealt with the tough issues throughout my life and what I learned to be true.

In describing the kind of leaders we need, I hope to address the difficult challenges that future leaders will face. First, I will describe authentic leaders and how they develop. Next, I will look at how authentic leaders build authentic companies, because that is the crux of leading. Third, I will show how authentic companies compete more effectively in the market, and, finally, how authentic leaders look beyond the bottom line. I hope to show all leaders, new and old alike, that there is a better way to lead than we have seen in the past decade—by pursuing your mission, living by your values, and getting superior results for all stakeholders. Now more than ever, we need to reflect on these issues.

Part One

Becoming an Authentic Leader

Leading an organization, large or small, is not an easy task. It can be lonely at times. Meeting the varied needs of the people you serve is a continuing struggle. Leaders are pulled in many different directions, yet must keep a clear vision of where they and their organizations are headed.

The complexities of twenty-first-century corporations demand new leadership. We need leaders who lead with purpose, values, and integrity and who are good stewards of the legacy they inherited from their predecessors. We need leaders who build enduring organizations, motivate their employees to provide superior customer service, and create long-term value for shareholders.

In short, we need a new kind of leader—*the authentic leader*—to bring us out of the current leadership crisis. My hope is that you will be inspired to become an authentic leader, committed to making the world better for all its citizens, and leading with your heart as well as your head.

Chapter One

Leadership Is Authenticity, Not Style

Something ignited in my soul,
Fever or unremembered wings,
And I went my own way,
Deciphering that burning fire.

—*Pablo Neruda*

Not long ago I was meeting with a group of high-talent young executives at Medtronic. We were discussing career development when the leader of the group asked me to list the most important characteristics one has to have to be a leader in Medtronic. I said, "I can summarize it in a single word: authenticity."

After years of studying leaders and their traits, I believe that leadership begins and ends with authenticity. It's being yourself; being the person you were created to be. This is not what most of the literature on leadership says, nor is it what the experts in corporate America teach. Instead, they develop lists of leadership characteristics one is supposed to emulate. They describe the styles of leaders and suggest that you adopt them.

This is the opposite of authenticity. It is about developing the image or *persona* of a leader. Unfortunately, the media, the business press, and even the movies glorify leaders with high-ego personalities. They focus on the style of leaders, not their character. In large measure, making heroes out of celebrity CEOs is at the heart of the crisis in corporate leadership.

The Authentic Leader

Authentic leaders genuinely desire to serve others through their leadership. They are more interested in empowering the people they lead to make a difference than they are in power, money, or prestige for themselves. They are as guided by qualities of the heart, by passion and compassion, as they are by qualities of the mind.

Authentic leaders are not born that way. Many people have natural leadership gifts, but they have to develop them fully to become outstanding leaders. Authentic leaders use their natural abilities, but they also recognize their shortcomings and work hard to overcome them. They lead with purpose, meaning, and values. They build enduring relationships with people. Others follow them because they know where they stand. They are consistent and self-disciplined. When their principles are tested, they refuse to compromise. Authentic leaders are dedicated to developing themselves because they know that becoming a leader takes a lifetime of personal growth.

Being Your Own Person

Leaders are all very different people. Any prospective leader who buys into the necessity of attempting to emulate all the characteristics of a leader is doomed to fail. I know because I tried it early in my career. It simply doesn't work.

The one essential quality a leader must have is to be your own person, authentic in every regard. The best leaders are autonomous and highly independent. Those who are too responsive to the desires of others are likely to be whipsawed by competing interests, too quick to deviate from their course or unwilling to make difficult decisions for fear of offending. My advice to the people I mentor is simply to be themselves.

Being your own person is most challenging when it feels like everyone is pressuring you to take one course and you are standing alone. In the first semester of business school we watched *The Lone-*

liness of the Long Distance Runner. Initially I did not relate to the film's message, as I had always surrounded myself with people to avoid being lonely. Learning to cope with the loneliness at the top is crucial so that you are not swayed by the pressure. Being able to stand alone against the majority is essential to being your own person.

Shortly after I joined Medtronic as president, I walked into a meeting where it quickly became evident that a group of my new colleagues had prearranged a strategy to settle a major patent dispute against Siemens on the basis of a royalty-free cross-license as a show of good faith. Intuitively, I knew the strategy was doomed to fail, so I stood alone against the entire group, refusing to go along. My position may not have made me popular with my new teammates, but it was the right thing to do. We later negotiated a settlement with Siemens for more than $400 million, at the time the second-largest patent settlement ever.

Developing Your Unique Leadership Style

To become authentic, each of us has to develop our own leadership style, consistent with our personality and character. Unfortunately, the pressures of an organization push us to adhere to its normative style. But if we conform to a style that is not consistent with who we are, we will never become authentic leaders.

Contrary to what much of the literature says, your type of leadership style is not what matters. Great world leaders—George Washington, Abraham Lincoln, Winston Churchill, Franklin Roosevelt, Margaret Thatcher, Martin Luther King, Mother Theresa, John F. Kennedy—all had very different styles. Yet each of them was an entirely authentic human being. There is no way you could ever attempt to emulate any of them without looking foolish.

The same is true for business leaders. Compare the last three CEOs of General Electric: the statesmanship of Reginald Jones, the dynamism of Jack Welch, and the empowering style of Jeff Immelt. All of them are highly successful leaders with entirely different leadership styles. Yet the GE organization has rallied around each of them, adapted to their styles, and flourished as a result. What counts is the authenticity of the leader, not the style.

Having said that, it is important that you develop a leadership style that works well for you and is consistent with your character and your personality. Over time you will have to hone your style to be effective in leading different types of people and to work in different types of environments. This is integral to your development as a leader.

To be effective in today's fast-moving, highly competitive environment, leaders also have to adapt their style to fit the immediate situation. There are times to be inspiring and motivating, and times to be tough about people decisions or financial decisions. There are times to delegate, and times to be deeply immersed in the details. There are times to communicate public messages, and times to have private conversations. The use of adaptive styles is not inauthentic, and is very different from playing a succession of roles rather than being yourself. Good leaders are able to nuance their styles to the demands of the situation, and to know when and how to deploy different styles.

Let me share a personal example to illustrate this point. When I first joined Medtronic, I spent a lot of time learning the business and listening to customers. I also focused on inspiring employees to fulfill the Medtronic mission of restoring people to full health. At the same time, I saw many ways in which we needed to be more disciplined about decisions and spending, so I was very challenging in budget sessions and put strict controls on headcount additions. At first some people found this confusing. Eventually, they understood my reasons for adapting my style to the situation, and that I had to do so to be effective as their leader.

Being Aware of Your Weaknesses

Being true to the person you were created to be means accepting your faults as well as using your strengths. Accepting your shadow side is an essential part of being authentic. The problem comes when people are so eager to win the approval of others that they try to cover their shortcomings and sacrifice their authenticity to gain the respect and admiration of their associates.

I too have struggled in getting comfortable with my weaknesses—my tendency to intimidate others with an overly challenging style, my impatience, and my occasional lack of tact. Only recently have I realized that my strengths and weaknesses are two sides of the same coin. By challenging others in business meetings, I am able to get quickly to the heart of the issues, but my approach unnerves and intimidates less confident people. My desire to get things done fast leads to superior results, but it exposes my impatience with people who move more slowly. Being direct with others gets the message across clearly but often lacks tact. Over time I have moderated my style and adapted my approach to make sure that people are engaged and empowered and that their voices are fully heard.

I have always been open to critical feedback, but also quite sensitive to it. For years I felt I had to be perfect, or at least appear that I was on top of everything. I tried to hide my weaknesses from others, fearing they would reject me if they knew who I really was. Eventually, I realized that they could see my weaknesses more clearly than I could. In attempting to cover things up, I was only fooling myself.

The poem "Love after Love," by Nobel Prize–winning poet Derek Walcott, speaks to the benefits of being in touch with your disowned aspects and welcoming them into your life. As I have been able to do so in recent years, I have become more comfortable with myself and more authentic in my interactions with others.

> *The time will come when with elation you will greet yourself,*
> *Arriving at your own door, in your own mirror,*
> *And each will smile at the other's welcome;*
> > *Saying, sit here. Eat.*
> *You will love again the stranger who was yourself.*
> *Give wine, give bread, give back your heart*

To the stranger who has loved all your life,
Whom you abandoned for another, who knows you by heart.
Take down the love letters from the bookshelf, the photographs,
  the desperate notes.
Sit. Feast on your life.

The Temptations of Leadership

Congressman Amory Houghton, one of the most thoughtful members of the U.S. Congress, tells the story of his predecessor's advice as he was taking over as CEO of Corning Glass. "Think of your decisions being based on two concentric circles. In the outer circle are all the laws, regulations, and ethical standards with which the company must comply. In the inner circle are your core values. Just be darn sure that your decisions as CEO stay within your inner circle."

We are all painfully aware of corporate leaders that pushed beyond the outer circle and got caught, either by the law or by the financial failure of their companies. More worrisome are the leaders of companies who moved outside their inner circles and engaged in marginal practices, albeit legal ones. Examples include cutting back on long-term investments just to make the short-term numbers, bending compensation rules to pay executives in spite of marginal performance, using accounting tricks to meet the quarterly expectations of security analysts, shipping products of marginal quality, compromising security analysts by giving them a cut on investment banking deals, and booking revenues before the products are shipped in an effort to pump up revenue growth. The list goes on and on.

All of us who sit in the leader's chair feel the pressure to perform. As CEO, I felt it every day as problems mounted or sales lagged. I knew that the livelihood of tens of thousands of employees, the health of millions of patients, and the financial fortunes of millions of investors rested on my shoulders and those of our executive team. At the same time I was well aware of the penalties for not performing, even for a single quarter. No CEO wants to appear on CNBC to explain why his company missed the earnings projections, even by a penny.

Little by little, step by step, the pressures to succeed can pull us away from our core values, just as we are reinforced by our "success" in the market. Some people refer to this as "CEO-itis." The irony is that the more successful we are, the more tempted we are to take shortcuts to keep it going. And the rewards—compensation increases, stock option gains, the myriads of executive perquisites, positive stories in the media, admiring comments from our peers— all reinforce our actions and drive us to keep it going.

In a recent interview with *Fortune* magazine, Novartis CEO Daniel Vasella talked about these pressures:

> Once you get under the domination of making the quarter—even unwittingly—you start to compromise in the gray areas of your business, that cut across the wide swath of terrain between the top and the bottom. Perhaps you'll begin to sacrifice things that are important and may be vital for your company over the long term. . . . The culprit that drives this cycle isn't the fear of failure so much as it is the craving for success. For the tyranny of quarterly earnings is a tyranny that is imposed from within. . . . For many of us the idea of being a successful manager is an intoxicating one. It is a pattern of celebration leading to belief, leading to distortion. When you achieve good results, you are typically celebrated, and you begin to believe that the figure at the center of all that champagne toasting is yourself. You are idealized by the outside world, and there is a natural tendency to believe that what is written is true.

Like Vasella, who is one of the finest and most authentic leaders I know, all leaders have to resist these pressures while continuing to perform, especially when things aren't going well. The test I used with our team at Medtronic is whether we would feel comfortable having the entire story appear on the front page of the *New York Times*. If we didn't, we went back to the drawing boards and re-examined our decision.

Dimensions of Authentic Leaders

Let's examine the essential dimensions of all authentic leaders, the qualities that true leaders must develop. I have determined through many experiences in leading others that authentic leaders demonstrate these five qualities:

- Understanding their purpose
- Practicing solid values
- Leading with heart
- Establishing connected relationships
- Demonstrating self-discipline

Acquiring the five dimensions of an authentic leader is not a sequential process; rather, leaders are developing them continuously throughout their lives. I think of them as five sections of a circle that blend together to form the authentic leader, as shown in Figure 1.1.

Figure 1.1 Dimensions of Authentic Leadership

Understanding Your Purpose

In Wonderland, Alice comes to a fork in the road where she sees a cat in a tree. Alice asks the cat, "Which road should I take?" "Do you know where you want to go?" inquires the cat. "No," says Alice. To which the cat replies, "Then any road will get you there."

To become a leader, it is essential that you first answer the question, "Leadership for what purpose?" If you lack purpose and direction in leading, why would anyone want to follow you?

Many people want to become leaders without giving much thought to their purpose. They are attracted to the power and prestige of leading an organization and the financial rewards that go with it. But without a real sense of purpose, leaders are at the mercy of their egos and are vulnerable to narcissistic impulses. There is no way you can adopt someone else's purpose and still be an authentic leader. You can study the purposes others pursue and you can work with them in common purposes, but in the end the purpose for your leadership must be uniquely yours.

To find your purpose, you must first understand yourself, your passions, and your underlying motivations. Then you must seek an environment that offers a fit between the organization's purpose and your own. Your search may take experiences in several organizations before you can find the one that is right for you.

The late Robert Greenleaf, a former AT&T executive, is well known for his concept of leaders as servants of the people. In *Servant Leadership*, he advocates service to others as the leader's primary purpose. If people feel you are genuinely interested in serving others, then they will be prepared not just to follow you but to dedicate themselves to the common cause.

One of the best examples of a leader with purpose was the late David Packard, co-founder of Hewlett-Packard. I met him in early 1969 when he was the new Deputy Secretary of Defense and I was the special assistant to the Secretary of Navy. Packard had taken a leave from H-P to serve his country. A big, powerful, yet modest man, he immediately impressed me with his openness, his sincerity, and his commitment to make a difference through his work.

He returned to H-P a few years later to build it into one of the great companies of its time through his dedication to the company's mission, known as "The H-P Way," and to excellence in R&D and customer service. He inspired H-P's employees to incredible levels of commitment. At his death he was one of the wealthiest people in the world, yet no one would ever have known it by his personal spending. Most of his money went into funding philanthropic projects. Dave Packard was a truly authentic leader, a role model for me and for many in my generation.

Then there's John Bogle, who for fifty years has been a man with a mission to transform the management of investors' funds. Bogle created the first no-load mutual fund in 1974 and founded Vanguard, the nation's leading purveyor of index funds. Bogle has not only been a pioneer in financial services, he has been the leading advocate of financial funds as stewards of their investors' money. His values and his integrity stand in stark relief with those in the financial community who seek to use investment funds for their personal gain.

Practicing Solid Values

Leaders are defined by their values and their character. The values of the authentic leader are shaped by personal beliefs, developed through study, introspection, and consultation with others—and a lifetime of experience. These values define their holder's moral compass. Such leaders know the "true north" of their compass, the deep sense of the right thing to do. Without a moral compass, any leader can wind up like the executives who are facing possible prison sentences today because they lacked a sense of right and wrong.

While the development of fundamental values is crucial, integrity is the one value that is required in every authentic leader. Integrity is not just the absence of lying, but telling the whole truth, as painful as it may be. If you don't exercise complete integrity in your interactions, no one can trust you. If they cannot trust you, why would they ever follow you?

I once had a colleague who would never lie to me, but often he shared only positive parts of the story, sheltering me from the ugly side. Finally, I told him that real integrity meant giving me the whole story so that together we could make sound decisions. Rather than thinking less of him if he did so, I assured him I would have a higher opinion of his courage and integrity.

Most business schools and academic institutions do not teach values as part of leadership development. Some offer ethics courses, often in a theoretical context, but shy away from discussing values. Others assume erroneously their students already have well-solidified values. What they fail to realize is the importance of solidifying your values through study and dialogue, and the impact that your environment has in shaping your values.

As Enron was collapsing in the fall of 2001, the *Boston Globe* published an article by a Harvard classmate of Enron CEO Jeff Skilling. The author described how Skilling would argue in class that the role of the business leader was to take advantage of loopholes in regulations and push beyond the laws wherever he could to make money. As Skilling saw the world, it was the job of the regulators to try and catch him. Sound familiar? Twenty-five years later, Skilling's philosophy caught up with him, as he led his company into bankruptcy.

One of my role models of values-centered leadership is Max DePree, the former CEO of furniture maker Herman Miller. DePree is a modest man guided by a deep concern for serving others; he is true to his values in every aspect of his life. His humanity and values can be seen through the exemplary way in which his company conducts itself. DePree describes his philosophy of values-centered leadership in his classic book, *Leadership Is an Art*. DePree also subscribes to Greenleaf's ideas on servant leadership, and expands them by offering his own advice, "The leader's first job is to define reality. The last is to say thank you. In between the leader must become a servant and a debtor."

DePree believes that a corporation should be "a community of people," all of whom have value and share in the fruits of their collective labor. DePree practices what he preaches. While he was CEO, his salary was capped at twenty times that of an hourly worker. In his view tying the CEO's salary to that of the workers helps cement trust in leadership. Contrast that with today's CEOs, who are earning—on average—five hundred times their hourly workers' wage. As DePree said recently, "When leaders indulge themselves with lavish perks and the trappings of power, they are damaging their standing as leaders."

Leading with Heart

Over the last several decades, businesses have evolved from maximizing the physical output of their workers to engaging the minds of their employees. To excel in the twenty-first century, great companies will go one step further by engaging the hearts of their employees through a sense of purpose. When employees believe their work has a deeper purpose, their results will vastly exceed those who use only their minds and their bodies. This will become the company's competitive advantage.

Sometimes we refer to people as being *bighearted*. What we really mean is that they are open and willing to share themselves fully with us, and are genuinely interested in us. Leaders who do that, like Sam Walton, founder of Wal-Mart, and Earl Bakken, founder of Medtronic, have the ability to ignite the souls of their employees to achieve greatness far beyond what anyone imagined possible.

One of the most bighearted leaders I know is Marilyn Nelson, chair and CEO of the Carlson Companies, the privately held hospitality and travel services giant. When she became CEO several years ago, she inherited a hard-nosed organization that was driven for growth but not known for empathy for its employees. Shortly after joining the company, Nelson had what she refers to as her "epiphany." She was meeting with the group of MBA students that had been studying the company's culture. When she asked the students for feedback, Nelson got a stony silence from the group. Finally, a young woman raised her hand and said, "We hear from employees that Carlson is a sweatshop that doesn't care."

That incident sent Nelson into high gear. She created a motivational program called "Carlson Cares." As the company was preparing for its launch, Nelson's staff told her they needed more time to change the culture before introducing the program. Nelson decided that she could not wait and decided to become the company's role model for caring and empathy. She immediately set out to change the environment, using her passion, motivational skills, and sincere interest in her employees and her customers. She took the lead on customer sales calls and interacted every day with employees in Carlson operations. Her positive energy has transformed the company's culture, built its customer relationships, accelerated its growth, and strengthened its bottom line.

Establishing Enduring Relationships

As Krishnamurti says, "Relationship is the mirror in which we see ourselves as we are."

The capacity to develop close and enduring relationships is one mark of a leader. Unfortunately, many leaders of major companies believe their job is to create the strategy, organization structure, and organizational processes. Then they just delegate the work to be done, remaining aloof from the people doing the work.

The detached style of leadership will not be successful in the twenty-first century. Today's employees demand more personal relationships with their leaders before they will give themselves fully to their jobs. They insist on having access to their leaders, knowing that it is in the openness and the depth of the relationship with the leader that trust and commitment are built. Bill Gates, Michael Dell, and Jack Welch are so successful because they connect directly with their employees and realize from them a deeper commitment to their work and greater loyalty to the company. Welch, in particular, is an interesting case because he was so challenging and hard on people. Yet it was those very challenges that let people know that he was interested in their success and concerned about their careers.

In *Eyewitness to Power*, David Gergen writes, "At the heart of leadership is the leader's relationship with followers. People will entrust their hopes and dreams to another person only if they think the other is a reliable vessel." Authentic leaders establish trusting relationships with people throughout the organization as well as in their personal lives. The rewards of these relationships, both tangible and intangible, are long lasting.

I always tried to establish close relationships with my colleagues, looking to them as a closely knit team whose collective knowledge and wisdom about the business vastly exceeds my own. Many corporate leaders fear these kinds of relationships. As another CEO said to me, "Bill, I don't want to get too close to my subordinates because someday I may have to terminate them." Actually, the real reason goes much deeper than that. Many leaders—men in particular—fear having their weaknesses and vulnerabilities exposed. So they create distance from employees and a sense of aloofness. Instead of being authentic, they are creating a persona for themselves.

Demonstrating Self-Discipline

Self-discipline is an essential quality of an authentic leader. Without it, you cannot gain the respect of your followers. It is easy to say that someone has good values but lacks the discipline to convert those values into consistent actions. This is a hollow excuse. None of us is perfect, of course, but authentic leaders must have the self-discipline to do everything they can to demonstrate their values through their actions. When we fall short, it is equally important to admit our mistakes.

Leaders are highly competitive people. They are driven to succeed in whatever they take on. Authentic leaders know that competing requires a consistently high level of self-discipline to be successful. Being very competitive is not a bad thing; in fact, it is an essential quality of successful leaders, but it needs to be channeled through purpose and discipline. Sometimes we mistake competitive people who generate near-term results by improving operational effectiveness for genuine leaders. Achieving operational effectiveness is an essential result for any leader, but it alone does not ensure authenticity or long-term success.

The most consistent leader I know is Art Collins, my successor as CEO of Medtronic. His self-discipline is evident every day and in every interaction. His subordinates never have to worry about what kind of mood Art is in, or where he stands on an important issue. Nor does he deviate in his behavior or vacillate in his decisions. He never lets his ego or his emotions get in the way of taking the appropriate action. These qualities make working with Art easy and predictable, enabling Medtronic employees to do their jobs effectively.

Mother Theresa is a compelling example of an authentic leader. Many think of her as simply a nun who reached out to the poor, yet by 1990 she had created an organization of four thousand missionaries operating in a hundred countries. Her organization, Missionaries of Charity, began in Calcutta and spread to 450 centers around the world. Its mission was "to reach out to the destitute on the streets, offering wholehearted service to the poorest of the poor." Not only did she have a purpose, clear values, and a heart filled with compassion, she also created intimate relationships with people and exercised self-discipline, all the dimensions of an authentic leader. I doubt that any of us will ever be like Mother Theresa, but her life is indeed an inspiration.

Chapter Two

The Transformation of Leaders

Ithaca does not exist; only the voyage to Ithaca.
—*Nikos Kazanzakis*

How do you become an authentic leader? In my experience it takes many years of personal development, experience, and just plain hard work. Although we may be born with leadership potential, all of us have to develop ourselves to become good leaders. The medium for developing into an authentic leader is not the destination but the journey itself—a journey to find your true self and the purpose of your life's work.

In the Crucible

In his recent book *Geeks and Geezers*, author Warren Bennis observes that most of his interviewees passed through a crucible that tested them to the depths of their being and enabled the successes they realized later in life. At some time in your journey you, too, may find yourself in a crucible that tests you to your limits. In this crucible you learn who you really are and what you want to become. Having survived, you will know that indeed you can take on any challenge and come out of it a better person for the experience.

My wife, Penny, experienced her crucible in 1996 when she was diagnosed with breast cancer. She went through a modified radical mastectomy, seven months of chemotherapy, five years of hormonal therapy, and a lifetime of not knowing whether the cancer would

27

recur. At first, she was convinced she was going to die. Gradually, she took back control of her life by creating her own healing path.

One of the steps on her journey was to participate in a Vision Quest in southwestern Utah. A Vision Quest is an experience based on the rituals of indigenous people in which participants seek to understand their purpose in the world. Fasting alone for four days and nights in the desert, Penny found a new power within herself and a renewed sense of purpose for her life. Several months afterward, she gave up her practice of psychology and devoted herself to the cause of integrative medicine, using the mind, body, heart, and spirit on one's healing journey. With passion and purpose, she is now working with medical leaders throughout the United States to change the way medicine is taught and practiced. Her inner power is enabling her to take on leadership roles she never believed she was capable of.

Four-time Tour de France winner Lance Armstrong makes a dramatic—almost unbelievable—statement in *It's Not About the Bike*, his book about his battle with life-threatening cancer. "The truth is, if you asked me to choose between winning the Tour de France and cancer, I would choose cancer." He goes on to explain, "Odd as it sounds, I would rather have the title of cancer survivor than winner of the Tour, because of what it has done for me as a human being, a man, a husband, a son, and a father."

Last fall I had the opportunity to bike with Lance up to the Maroon Bells near Aspen and to ask him about his views on cancer. He explained how his battle with cancer had transformed him as a person and opened up his opportunities for marriage, fatherhood, and, yes, had given him the focus and discipline to win the Tour four times in a row. He told me he wrote the book not to glorify his achievements—"those will soon be forgotten"—but to give hope to millions of cancer sufferers.

Shooting Stars and Golden Boys

Some rising leaders avoid challenging experiences that really test them. I refer to them as Shooting Stars and Golden Boys. The Shooting Stars move up so rapidly they never take time to learn from their mistakes or look at themselves in the mirror. A year or two into any job, they are ready to move on, long before they have to pass the test of living with their decisions. When they see an experience like the crucible coming, their anxiety rises and so does the urgency to move on. If their employer doesn't move them upward, they are off to the next company. Then some day they find themselves at the top, confronted with an overwhelming set of problems. Without the wisdom of the crucible, they cannot cope and are prone to do bizarre things on their way to self-destruction.

Golden Boys (and Girls) follow a similar path to success, using charm, style, and good looks to get ahead. They always set the bar of performance low enough to ensure that they can exceed it. To outsiders and board members, they always appear in control. Insiders observe that a Golden Boy never gets his hands dirty wrestling with problems. When he reaches the top, he is unprepared for the real-world challenges he will encounter. When faced with them, he is vulnerable to making major mistakes and putting his company at risk.

My Journey to Leadership

On my journey I went through several experiences in the crucible before I developed into the kind of leader I had always dreamt of becoming. In my early years I was hardly recognized as a leader by my peers. I was not the one to be elected to the student council or to captain the tennis team. There was a simple reason for this. I was so ambitious and self-centered that I never took the time to develop close relationships.

In my desire to become a leader, I studied the biographies of world leaders, as well as great business leaders of my era, attempting to develop the leadership characteristics they displayed. It didn't work. I was more of a persona than an authentic leader. No wonder my early attempts at leadership failed. In high school I ran for president of the senior class, only to lose by a two-to-one margin. I was devastated. I had not yet learned what it takes to have people want to follow you.

Through my college fraternity, I got some wonderful coaching from upperclassmen about the way in which my self-centeredness was a barrier to relationships with others. Even so, I lost six consecutive elections in the fraternity before I came to grips with my shortcomings and began to focus on others instead of myself. As I got in touch with my weaknesses and gradually became more authentic, I was chosen to lead many organizations.

During my career I received lots of feedback to modify my leadership style so as to fit in with the organization's norms. Several supervisors and human resource specialists urged me to become a different kind of leader: less passionate, more laid back, less engaged, less challenging, less critical of others. I listened carefully to their advice but quietly rejected it. Had I followed this advice, I would have become a "plain vanilla" manager or even been seen as a phony. It would have taken away my best qualities to moderate my leadership style, just to make others feel more comfortable. This may be a good quality for middle managers but not for those in top leadership. As a team-building consultant once said to me, "Bill, working with you is no day at the beach!"

It took me twenty years in business to find the right place to devote my energies—a mission-driven company named Medtronic. Had it not been for the frustrations of my previous job, I might never have accepted the opportunity. It turned out to be the most important step of my career.

Coping with Tragedy

Bad things happen in life that we cannot anticipate. Rabbi Harold Kushner has written thoughtfully about how bad things happen to good people. In my mid-twenties I had my experience in the crucible, one for which I was fully unprepared. Two tragedies brought me face-to-face with the meaning of life, its pain, and its injustices.

After graduating from business school, I went to work in Washington and was feeling on top of the world. I loved my work, my friends, and my new environment. Then one day I received an emergency telephone call. My father was on the line. He could barely speak as he told me that my mother had died that morning of a sudden heart attack. I was closer to her than to anyone else in the world. She was my role model, my supporter, my ally, and the person from whom I learned unconditional love.

When I arrived home later that afternoon, my father met me at the door. I will never forget our interaction. Looking into his eyes, I knew instantly that I had to become the father of my father. This role reversal continued for the last twenty-five years of his life. In a very real sense I lost two parents in one day. At age twenty-four I became the elder. As is said, "The son becomes the father of the man."

Not long after mother's death, I fell in love and got engaged. Just a few weeks before the wedding, my fiancée started to experience severe headaches, double vision, and loss of sense of balance. I was so worried that I took her to a leading neurosurgeon, who put her into the hospital for a week of neurological tests. All her exams were negative, but the severe headaches continued. The neurosurgeon told us rather coldly that my fiancée was emotionally disturbed about getting married. He sent her to her parents' home in Georgia to see a psychologist.

Intuitively, I knew this was a misdiagnosis. Something was seriously wrong with my fiancée, but it was definitely not a psychological problem. I did not know where to turn for help. The wedding was just three weeks away, and we had still not sent out the invitations. We talked by telephone on a Saturday night but were paralyzed about what to do next.

The following morning I returned home from church, where I'd been praying for my fiancée's recovery. Our large Georgetown house was dark and the curtains were pulled, which seemed odd for a sunny August morning. One of my roommates met me at the door and asked me to sit down in the living room. I immediately sensed the worst, exclaiming, "She's not dead, is she?" He nodded affirmatively. She had died that morning in her father's arms, the victim of a malignant brain tumor. I felt shock and searing pain as once again

I tumbled into the well of grief. I felt completely alone in the world and unable to comprehend the deeper meaning of what had just happened. Thankfully, my friends gathered around me that day and in the weeks that followed and provided the love and support I so desperately needed. To them I will be forever grateful.

This was a crucial time in my life when I could have easily become bitter, depressed, and even lost my faith. In times of personal crisis, the grace of God and the power of faith can provide the basis for healing. So can the support of friends. I was blessed to have both. Together they gave me hope for the future and enabled me not to feel sorry for myself, just for my fiancée and her family. I came to the realization that there are many things in life we cannot understand and may never be able to explain. The words of St. Paul provided the greatest comfort, "Now we see through a glass darkly. Then, face to face."

Tragic as these events were, they opened my heart to the deeper meaning of life, and got me thinking more profoundly about what I could contribute to others during my lifetime.

"Hitting the Wall"

"In the middle of the road of my life, I awoke in a dark wood, where the true way was wholly lost" Dante writes in *The Divine Comedy*.

My most agonizing time in the career crucible also came when I least expected it. I call this "hitting the wall," something that happens to most leaders at least once in their careers. As painful as it was, this experience provided the basis for growth and change that transformed my career. It caused me to look inside myself, acknowledge my shortcomings, and realize I was on the wrong path.

In the mid-1980s I was on my way to the top of Honeywell. What began as a huge promotion turned into a decision to reassess my career and to move in an entirely new direction. By 1988 I had been promoted several times, each time taking over more responsibility for Honeywell's most challenging businesses. At the time I was responsible for three groups, nine divisions, eighteen thousand employees, and a raft of problems.

I had developed a reputation as "Mr. Fixit," the guy who could get Honeywell's troubled businesses turned around. I knew *how* to turn businesses around, but I never got the opportunity to reap the fruits of my labor before moving on to the next set of troubled operations. In my last assignment, I uncovered losses approaching $400 million that had not been recognized or accounted for properly. This caused a great deal of consternation for the Honeywell board and its shareholders. There was nothing we could do except get all the problems on the table and correct them. As I was fond of saying, "I didn't create these problems. I'm just the guy who's getting them fixed."

During this period I started questioning whether Honeywell was really the place for me. I have always seen myself as a growth-oriented leader, not a turnaround specialist. When presented with problems, I was quite willing to take responsibility for them and get them resolved, but I also yearned to experience the fruits of my labor.

My lack of passion for Honeywell's businesses also troubled me. I was out of sync with Honeywell's slow-moving, change-resistant culture. I also found myself becoming more concerned with appearances and my attire than with being myself. Reluctantly, I faced up to the reality that Honeywell was changing me more than I was changing it.

I had "hit the wall," but was too proud to face it. I felt I was in a trap from which I couldn't escape. The macho side of me said, "I have to tough it out." Sure, I was leading, but the purpose of my efforts was not at all clear. Where was my "leading" leading to?

On a beautiful fall afternoon when the maple trees were blazing red, I had a daydream while driving around the lake near my home. But this dream was not pretty. I saw myself staying at Honeywell for a few more years, becoming increasingly frustrated, and then deciding to accept a CEO position at a large company in some other city. This would mean uprooting my family, Penny giving up her job, our sons changing schools, all of us leaving the community we loved. Why would I do that? Just to satisfy my ego? I had a lot of self-explanation to do.

My experience that day enabled me to realize that, like Dante, I too was "in a dark wood." I needed to wake up and overcome my fixation on being CEO of a very large corporation. Reluctantly, I realized I was letting my ego get in the way of my values. If indeed I was in a trap, it was a trap of my own making. When we are in this position, it is difficult to see things clearly, and we may miss the opportunity that is staring us in the face.

Over the years I had had three opportunities to join Medtronic, dating back to 1978. I turned them all down, mostly because I didn't feel Medtronic was a large enough company for me. Yet the opportunity kept nagging at me. Had I done the right thing? It finally dawned on me that I was so caught up in my drive to run a major corporation that I was in danger of losing my soul. In the process I realized I had sold Medtronic short, and maybe myself as well. That evening Penny and I had a long talk about our lives and our careers. We recognized that my lack of fulfillment in my job was having a negative impact on all of us. She encouraged me to take another look at Medtronic.

I kept thinking about the vision I had in my teenage years: leading a mission-driven, values-centered company where I was passionate about the company's products and the opportunity to serve others. What better place to do that than Medtronic? I called Medtronic's CEO and reopened the door. Five months later I walked through Medtronic's door to become its president and chief operating officer. Rarely in life does opportunity knock four times.

Finding the Right Place

I finally had found the place—or it had found me—that offered everything I wanted: values, passion, and the opportunity to help people suffering from chronic disease. Had it not been for my experience in the crucible, I might never have seen the light. I have never looked back nor regretted it. It was only in going my own way I became fully alive and developed my potential as a leader.

Throughout my life I have had a passion to make a difference in the world. At Medtronic I was able to lead a company that changes people's lives. I feel a deep sense of good fortune in finding a confluence of interests between my personal desires and the needs of Medtronic. The Medtronic mission to restore people to fuller health inspired me from the moment Medtronic founder Earl Bakken described it to me. Fourteen years later, it inspires me even more.

I don't want to oversimplify the challenges of leading a rapidly growing organization. Being the leader is a tough job with a lot of pressure that can arise at any moment from an unanticipated source. There was rarely a time when I could put aside thoughts about my work and focus entirely on other things. With all the challenges we faced, it was inevitable that I had fears and doubts. As good as my subordinates were, I knew the final decision—and the lives of thousands of people—rested in my hands, my head, and my heart.

Over the years we faced continuous challenges from a wide range of sources. Looking back, I made some good decisions, but also made my share of mistakes. The thrill of taking on these challenges with a team of people I deeply respected was worth every ounce of stress. During these years I often felt like Theodore Roosevelt's "Man in the Arena,"

> Whose face is marred by dust and sweat and blood; who strives valiantly . . . who knows the great enthusiasms, the great devotions; who spends himself in a worthy cause; who at the best knows in the end the triumph of high achievement, and who at the worst, if he fails, at least fails while daring greatly so that his place shall never be with those cold and timid souls who have never known neither victory nor defeat.

Underpinning everything I have done in life is a strong faith. My experiences, both good and bad, have only served to strengthen the conviction gained in my younger years that a loving God is there to guide me along the way through all the difficulties I may encounter.

Developing as an Authentic Leader

Let's return to the five dimensions of authentic leadership and explore how leaders develop themselves in each area. As shown in Figure 2.1, for each of the dimensions, a developmental quality is required for leaders to be effective:

- *Purpose:* Passion
- *Values:* Behavior
- *Heart:* Compassion
- *Relationships:* Connectedness
- *Self-Discipline:* Consistency

Passion for Your Purpose

Many leaders search for years, even decades, to find the purpose for their leadership. It is relatively easy to state your purpose early in life, but much harder to develop passion for it. Passion for your pur-

Figure 2.1 The Authentic Leader's Characteristics

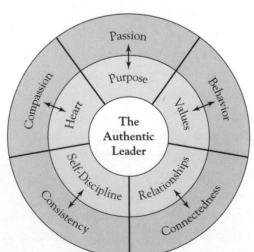

pose comes when you are highly motivated by your work because you believe in its intrinsic worth, and you can use your abilities to maximum effect.

If your early career experiences do not inspire you, then it is wise to continue your search in a different venue, job, or company where you can find passion for your work. After all, life goes by quickly and you don't want to spend your time sleepwalking through life.

Earl Bakken, the founder of Medtronic, expresses more passion for the mission of his company than any person I have ever met. Earl started the company in 1949 in his brother-in-law's garage, where the company had its headquarters for the next twelve years. Responding to an urgent request in 1957 from Dr. C. Walton Lillihei, the creator of open-heart surgery, Earl invented the world's first wearable pacemaker. In spite of that success, five years later Medtronic was still losing money, out of cash, and nearing bankruptcy. At the urging of his board of directors to bring focus to the company, Earl wrote the Medtronic mission "to restore people to fuller lives." The mission convinced a local venture capitalist to provide the funding to keep the company going. The rest, as they say, is history.

Every time Earl talks to employees or customers, he describes the mission and enlists them to his cause. He carries a supply of cards with the mission written on it in his pocket, and gives these cards out to everyone he meets. He frequently shares stories of patients whose lives have been restored by Medtronic products. It is hard not to get caught up by his passion.

Being True to Your Values

Having found the purpose that ignites your passions, you then have to test your values in the crucible of life's experiences. This doesn't just happen by listing your values. Only in the crucible will you learn how to cope with pressures to compromise your values and deal with potential conflicts between them. You have to put yourself in situations in which your values are challenged and then make difficult decisions in the context of your values. This is not easy when the outcome is uncertain and there is a lot at stake.

Nonetheless, it is in these situations and not the easy ones that you find the "true north" of your moral compass.

When asked about their ethics, most leaders espouse solid values. Many of them meet regularly with their employees and implore them to practice these values or risk losing their jobs. Under pressure, these same leaders may behave in an entirely different manner. There is nothing worse than leaders who preach good values but fail to follow their own advice, or who set double standards for their employees and themselves. If you want to see employees become cynical, just watch what happens when the top executives behave in ways inconsistent with company values. For one example, look at Dennis Koslowski, former CEO of Tyco, who set up an endowed chair in corporate governance at Cambridge University in the United Kingdom just as he was demolishing any semblance of sound governance on his own board.

Having your values tested early in life, when the stakes are lower, can be formative in your development. Here's an example of an early values test a young friend of mine experienced. The day after he was elected president of his college fraternity, his treasurer presented him with a serious problem. The former treasurer had dropped out of school and left the fraternity with a $6,000 shortfall. As a result, funds were not adequate to provide meals for the rest of the year and all social events would have to be cancelled. Not to worry, said the treasurer, he had a solution: temporarily use the $6,000 the chapter had raised for a charity that aids orphans, as the money wasn't due for several months. All the other officers and graduating seniors supported the treasurer's proposal.

The young president agonized for several days as the pressures on him mounted to go along with the majority. Finally, he called the group together and told them that he could not support it. How could he look himself in the mirror, knowing that he had borrowed from the orphans' funds to meet operating expenses? What would happen to their reputation if the word leaked out on campus that they had used these funds? Instead, he asked the other three officers to go with him to the local bank and to take out loans of $1,500 each to cover the shortfall until the coffers were refilled.

That is integrity in action. Someday when the stakes are higher and this young leader is under great pressure, the wisdom of his experience in the crucible will speak to him.

Finding a company where there is a solid fit between your values and the organization's values is more difficult than it sounds. Often it takes a crisis before you realize how people will behave under pressure and what their real values are. The important takeaway is not to let your values be compromised by the organization. You may have to acknowledge that the values of others in the organization do not match yours, but that is no reason for sacrificing your beliefs just to get ahead. People will respect you for being true to your values and be willing to follow you.

Developing Compassion

Can you lead authentically without compassion? Not really, although some leaders behave as though they have no compassion for anyone. It is your life experiences that open up your heart to have compassion for the most difficult challenges that people face along life's journey. Far too many leaders wall themselves off from people who are experiencing the full range of life's challenges, hardships, and difficulties. Instead, they prefer the comfort of being with people like themselves. They often avoid intimate relationships, even with their friends and loved ones.

Unfortunately, the trends in our society of attending private schools, avoiding military service, and being too busy in our careers to get involved in our communities shield us from the very experiences that open up our hearts. Every day we have opportunities to develop our hearts, through getting to know the life stories of those with whom we work, taking on community service projects, having international students living in our homes, understanding the roots of discrimination, and traveling through developing countries and understanding the lives of their people.

We can also develop compassion through intimate relationships with family, friends, and coworkers, and having mentoring relationships. Through the connections formed through personal sharing, people are inspired to believe in their leaders and follow them.

Recently I shared with Dan Vasella of Novartis the struggles the spouse of a Medtronic employee was having with Stage IV breast cancer, but did not ask him for his help. Nevertheless, Dan responded immediately with the sensitivity of a great physician and the compassion of a true leader. The employee and his spouse were deeply moved by his caring.

At my Medtronic going-away event a longtime colleague described me as "a leader who would be remembered for his passion and compassion." He went on to describe instances illustrating those qualities in the workplace, including the day he had called to tell me that his son had just been diagnosed with terminal stomach cancer, and I immediately drove to the hospital, where we embraced and shared some tears and prayers in the hall outside his son's room.

No one could have paid me a greater compliment. For much of my career I was known as a driven leader, able to see quickly to the heart of a difficult issue and get it resolved. To be recognized for qualities of the heart was the most meaningful tribute I can imagine.

Developing your heart means following your own path and being open to all of life's experiences. It means being in touch with the depths of your inner being and being true to yourself. It requires that you know who you are, your weaknesses as well as your strengths. It is in developing compassion that we become authentic human beings.

Connected Relationships

Enduring relationships are built on connectedness and a shared purpose of working together toward a common goal. Every person has a life story they want to share with you, if you are open to hearing their story and sharing with them. It is in sharing our life stories that we develop trust and intimacy with our colleagues.

Leaders who are open with people, even when sharing bad news or offering critical feedback, establish that sense of connection that builds commitment. Trust is built and sustained in the depths of these relationships, and commitment is strengthened so that any obstacle can be overcome. When pressures mount, relationships built on connectedness actually grow.

It took me several years to establish deep relationships at Medtronic, to build the trust of all our employees, and to let people get to know who I am and what I believe in. My experience with my wife's breast cancer quite unexpectedly opened up those relationships. By Thanksgiving of that year Penny was finally on her journey to healing, having completed her chemotherapy. I sent an e-mail message to all Medtronic employees worldwide describing our gratitude for her recovery and all the support we had received from Medtronic employees during the year. The response was overwhelming and completely unexpected. Hundreds of Medtronic employees from all over the world responded with their own e-mail thanking me for my openness and sharing their own stories of personal traumas. This stream of e-mail continued for several years. Looking back on their responses, I believe they indicate just how much people desire that kind of connectedness with their leaders.

Practicing Self-Discipline

Leaders are always being examined under the microscope. Their behaviors are observed, discussed, and dissected by their employees as well as by a myriad of outsiders. Are they having a good day? How will they respond to my proposal? Will they issue pink slips today? Do I dare share these problems with my boss?

To be authentic, leaders must behave with consistency and self-discipline, not letting stress get in the way of their judgment. They must learn to handle any kind of pressure and stay cool and calm. Handling unexpected challenges requires being in peak condition. Like a professional athlete, they need consistent habits to keep their minds sharp and their bodies in shape.

Without presuming what may work for you, let me share what I do to relieve the stresses of leadership. Twenty-five years ago I took up meditation and have meditated twice a day ever since. Meditation helps clear away my trivial thoughts and worries, enables me to focus on the important things, and gives me added energy to get through a stressful day. Many of my most creative ideas come as I am concluding my meditations.

By having a daily exercise routine and engaging in strenuous exercise at least three to four times a week, I am more effective at work. Consistent eating patterns, with an emphasis on a balanced, low-fat diet, are the best way to have good health and plenty of energy to be fully productive. Regular sleep patterns are also crucial to being sharp on the job. I fail to understand young professionals and corporate leaders who work sixteen hours a day or more. I know I couldn't make good decisions without adequate sleep and some relief from the workplace.

There are many other ways to relieve anxieties, such as discussions with your spouse, prayer, laughter, celebrations, movies, sport-

---

The leadership book that had the greatest influence on me is Warren Bennis's *On Becoming a Leader*. Warren writes about the importance of passion, compassion, vision, and vitality in a leader, characteristics that rang true to me, that I tried to cultivate at Medtronic. Two years ago I learned that Warren had received a Medtronic defibrillator, so I invited him to the Medtronic Holiday Party, an annual event where people who have our products implanted in them come to relate their stories and reinforce the importance of the work of our employees. Warren was the ideal participant; before receiving the defibrillator, the drugs he was taking were so debilitating that it was extremely difficult for him to teach and write. Now—at age seventy-seven—he is going stronger than ever, teaching both at Harvard and Southern California and giving talks about his new book, *Geeks and Geezers.*

ing events, reading, and relaxation. The particulars of stress reduction are a matter of individual choice, but the important thing is to have consistent habits that provide self-discipline.

Developing these qualities of the authentic leader—purpose, behavior, compassion, connectedness, consistency—takes many years of journeying through life's experiences. It is a never-ending process. The rewards lie not only in being a better leader, but having a fulfilling life.

Reflections on the Journey

Several years ago Penny and I were at a conference in San Francisco and decided to walk the labyrinth in the nave of Grace Cathedral. In the labyrinth you start in the outer circle, but the path takes you quickly toward the center, which appears to be the purpose of your walk. As you are about to reach the center, the path turns away and you walk toward the outside. Around the perimeter, sometimes closer, sometimes farther away. Just as you are about to give up on ever reaching the center, the path turns toward the center and suddenly you are there!

The labyrinth is exhilarating, and also highly instructive. The journey itself is the message. Often the most important things you learn in life come when you seem to be going nowhere, or actually backward. This is the way it has been on my leadership journey.

When I graduated from business school, I envisioned a straight-line career, progressing to the top of a major corporation. For the next twenty years, I was moving steadily in that direction. I believed my big promotion within Honeywell was another important step along that path. Little did I realize at that point just how much I had to learn about leadership, about myself, and about life.

When my path turned away from the center, I felt I was "wandering through the Gobi desert," without signposts and without an oasis. Other times I felt like I was beating my head against a stone wall. It was not a lot of fun. In retrospect, though, this was a crucial learning experience. Looking back over that period, I realize now—with the benefit of 20/20 hindsight—that experiencing such a difficult time at work was an essential part of my development and later success. But it is hard to recognize it when you're in the midst of endless problems and seventy-hour weeks.

My greatest joy in work has come in organizing a group of people to build something of real importance and great meaning. My years in the crucible gave me the courage to follow my heart and use my motivated abilities. They also helped me realize what is most important in life—not just career success, but also my marriage, our sons, and being part of a community. Joining Medtronic enabled me to get back to my roots and into an environment that would value me for who I was, not just what I could accomplish.

Becoming an authentic leader involves many years of hard work, some pain and suffering, and the wisdom that comes from experiencing life at its fullest. It is only in the labyrinth and crucible of life that we develop into authentic leaders.

Chapter Three

Leading a Balanced Life

But yield who will to their separation,
My object in living is to unite
My avocation and my vocation
As my two eyes make one in sight.
          —*Robert Frost, "Two Tramps in Mud Time"*

Are you interested in more from life than your work? I certainly hope so. As much time as we devote to our work, nearly every one of us wants to experience the full breadth that life has to offer. Yet our behaviors often suggest that our work is our life, or at least that it takes priority over everything else.

Regrettably, the role models in our parents' generation are not good. Many of these leaders felt the company was their life. Listen to what Robert Crandall, retired chairman and CEO of American Airlines, said on this subject in *Geeks and Geezers:*

> For all the years that I was working, I was trying to achieve a particular goal. So I wasn't interested in balance. I didn't sail very much. I didn't play any golf. I didn't take much time off. I ran American Airlines and it pretty much took up my whole life. Which suited me fine. . . . Now you hear a lot about balance. In today's world people say, "I have to have a more balanced life. I have to have time for my kids and my job and my hobbies." That's all well and good. But people who worry about balance have no overriding passion to achieve leadership.

As much as I respect what Crandall accomplished at American, I disagree completely on his views about balance and passion. His voice is that of another era, when men worked and their wives supported them from their homes. If you follow his advice, you may become a very narrow person and a limited leader. At the end of the day you could wind up with few followers and even fewer friends.

A Balanced Life Makes You a Better Leader

Let's confront directly the notion of who are the better leaders: the eighty-hours-per-week executives who live for work and subordinate everything to the company's perceived needs, or the leaders who work equally hard during fifty to sixty hours but balance their work with the needs of their families?

Balanced leaders develop healthier organizations. By appropriately delegating their work, balanced leaders are able to make more thoughtful decisions and lead more effectively. Their employees make higher levels of commitment to the organization. In the end they achieve better results on the bottom line.

Contrary to what Crandall says, my leadership flourished when I found congruence between my work, my personal life, and the company's mission. Today's emerging leaders know from experiences in their own families that balance is imperative for leading a fulfilling life. They are committed to excelling in their work, but they know that there is much more to life. They certainly do not lack the passion to lead. Quite the contrary: they will be better leaders *because* they are living balanced lives.

If we sell our souls to the company, at the end of the day we may find we have little to show for our efforts. If we seek organizations that nourish our souls, enable us to grow into fully functioning human beings, and connect us with fellow wayfarers, we can live a full life.

Being Authentic in All Aspects of Your Life

Being authentic is not just something you are at work. It must be reflected in all aspects of your life. Unfortunately, the pressures of society and work life often cause us to behave differently in the various aspects of life—work, family, social, spiritual. As a result, we wind up compartmentalizing our lives.

Can you imagine yourself trying to be a strong, mature leader at work, impervious to all the pressures? A rising, sophisticated leader in your community? A loving, laid-back person at home? And attempting to practice a private spiritual life? That's what I was doing in my early thirties. The only way I could cope with all these different roles was to create internal compartments for each of them and behave according to the expectations I encountered in each environment. Of course, anyone who knew me well saw that I was anything but authentic in these roles.

Then Penny and I went to a weekend called Cursillo, put on by the laypeople of the Episcopal Church. Cursillo (short for the Spanish *Cursillo de Cristiandad*, which means "short course in Christianity") was a life-changing experience for us. We were deeply moved by the sharing of Christian love that we experienced throughout the weekend.

During this weekend I saw clearly for the first time how I was compartmentalizing my life. I did not have the courage to share all of myself and who I really was with people in these different environments, especially my superiors at work. I was so afraid to tell my boss at Litton where I was going that I set up a special arrangement with my secretary to contact me if he called. Being on the golf course would not have been a problem, but a religious retreat?

Coming out of Cursillo, I resolved to knock down these artificial walls and "decompartmentalize" my life. My commitment to myself was to be the same person at home, at work, in the community, and in church. During this time Penny was a great reality check, challenging me when she observed me behaving differently in social settings, for example, and talking with me about how I could change. This was not easy. It took me many years of effort before I could make these interior walls disappear and let people in every aspect of my life know who I really was.

Work and Family Life

These days the most important question on the minds of developing leaders is, "Can I have a great career *and* a great family life?" I get asked this all the time from the people I am mentoring and my MBA students. The challenge of finding that delicate balance is greater today than it ever has been, due to increasing pressures and time demands on the job and the complexities of two-career marriages. Today's rising leaders have seen many people in their parents' generation sacrifice their families for their careers, and have lived through the pain of broken marriages and estranged relationships. They are committed to doing it differently, but often they don't know how.

Finding a balance between your work and home life is one of the most difficult issues any leader faces. There are no clear answers, and you must make continual trade-offs. Most of us want to have a successful career and a comfortable and rewarding marriage and family life. That is certainly admirable. The problem comes when you get into the habit of sacrificing yourself and your family for the company. Years later you may find yourself in a career trap that you can't extract yourself from because your living expenses are so high you can't afford to quit. Yet you may not realize the trap in the early stages of your career. My advice is to establish clear ground rules for your work-home life balance and stick to them, rather than getting into the habit of "doing whatever it takes" to get ahead.

When I was at Litton, my boss was one of the top five people in the company; he owned an expensive home in Beverly Hills and belonged to exclusive country clubs. Yet he called regularly to tell me how much he hated his job. One day I finally said to him, "If it's that bad, why don't you quit?" Instantly he replied, "With all my expenses, I can't afford to." A few years later, he died of lung cancer from smoking to relieve his stress. No one ever knew what happened to all the money he was making.

To find that delicate balance, it is essential to set clear boundaries between work and home life. If you do so, you will be pleasantly surprised about where life will lead you. After all, the alternative is to earn a lot of money and not have the time to share it with your family, or to become estranged from your spouse and children because you neglected them.

Managing Dual Careers

From the time I was a teenager, I was committed to leading a great organization *and* having a great family life. I had friends whose fathers sacrificed their families to excel in their careers. I worried a lot about this happening in my life. When Penny and I were dating, we talked about how we could support both our careers and still have plenty of time for our family. At that stage we had no experience with children of our own, and I was rather naive about the time requirements of raising children. Before our children were born, finding a balance was pretty easy. With both of us working, we were still able to adapt our schedules and spend our nonworking hours together.

When our sons, Jeff and Jon, were born, everything changed. Penny was working as a consulting psychologist after obtaining her master's degree in psychology. She took time off from her job after each boy was born and then went back to work part time. Meanwhile, the intensity of my work was heating up, as I was traveling regularly to Japan and Europe, sometimes on trips spanning ten days at a time. My absences put a lot of pressure on Penny to raise the boys *and* get her work done.

I tried to do my full share of the child rearing, the chores, and the boys' transportation to day care or to sports, as well as carry my share of the emotional load. I cannot say that I succeeded. Hard as I tried, Penny wound up with a much greater share of the burden, especially when I was traveling. These days I am a lot more realistic about the trade-offs involved.

"Hitting the Wall" at Home

Marriage is *not* a static state. To have a successful long-term marriage, you and your spouse have to work at it continually, talking openly about your differences, your fears, and your vulnerabilities.

Penny has been the barometer in our relationship, forcing us to talk through the issues when we seem to be drifting apart or too caught up in our own worlds. This has been an enormous help to me in opening up more.

Not surprisingly, the high stress at Honeywell I experienced in the late 1980s also carried over into my home life. During those years I was traveling almost constantly, which was very hard on both Penny and me. I found myself less and less happy with my work and began turning to activities outside the company for a sense of fulfillment. Meanwhile, I was in denial about how the stress was affecting my family and me.

It was a good thing Penny confronted me about my behavior and the stress it was putting on her and the boys. We survived that period, but it wasn't easy. Moving to Medtronic not only was more satisfying to me personally, it also made life better for Penny and the boys. When you are feeling under a great deal of pressure, it is often hard to recognize its impact on those closest to you. In retrospect, it took pain at work *and* at home for me to face up to the reality that I needed to change directions in my career and focus on what is really important in life.

Finding That Delicate Balance

It is important to recognize that in any relationship, both people are growing and changing, quite likely in different ways. This mandates careful monitoring and communication about the relationship. Paying attention to these issues early in life can save a lot of heartaches later on. Looking back on our parenting years, I can see that Penny and I should have talked about the trade-offs between work and home life before we had children.

Kris Johnson, a former Medtronic executive, is an example of an effective leader who has worked hard to find that delicate balance, along with her husband, Rob, a senior executive at Cargill. When I joined the company, Kris was the star of Medtronic's corporate staff. She then built Medtronic's defibrillator business for six crucial years before becoming president of the vascular business. Throughout this time Kris was extremely dedicated to her two daughters and actively engaged in their lives. At a certain point Kris decided that the pressure of international travel was pulling her away too frequently from her family. She shifted to venture capital work, where she has better control over her schedule. Not surprisingly, she is doing very well in her new work *and* she has achieved that solid balance in her home life.

The key to keeping your work and home life in balance is to examine it continually, be conscious of the trade-offs, and make adjustments as necessary for the sake of your loved ones. While there are no easy answers here, with real effort you can have the satisfaction of a great marriage and family life *and* an outstanding career.

Raising a Family

Raising our two sons has been one of the greatest joys of our lives. Jeff and Jon have very different personalities—"the yin and the yang" as Penny calls them—yet they share a common set of values and are good friends. After the usual adolescent challenges, they are both launched, Jeff into the consulting business and Jon into medical school.

From listening to the boys and observing their growth, I have learned a great deal about life and about myself. For successful fathers, raising sons without imposing your ideas and career standards on them can be a challenge. I was determined not to repeat some of the mistakes my father made and to encourage the boys to pursue whatever paths they chose. The best advice on raising children comes from Kahlil Gibran, in *The Prophet:*

> *Your children are not your children.*
> *They are the son and daughters of Life's longing for itself.*
> *You may give them your love but not your thoughts,*
> *For they have their own thoughts.*
> *You may house their bodies but not their souls,*

For their souls dwell in the house of tomorrow,
Which you cannot visit, not even in your dreams.
You may strive to be like them, but seek not to make them like you.
For life goes not backwards, nor tarries with yesterday.

These days my sons and I are moving away from the parent-child relationship and maturing into deep friendships. We take trips together to Alaska and Sea Pines, climb 14,000-foot peaks in the Colorado Rockies, and discuss everything from girlfriends to career issues. My sons also give me some great advice on living more fully in the moment.

Friendships

At the end of the day, what is more important than your family and your friends? With friends of many years, you develop the special bond of shared life histories. However, friendships need to be nurtured and cannot be taken for granted. In general, women are much better at cultivating friendships than men are and share more intimately with their friends. All too often, men limit their friendships to golfing and drinking buddies and rarely share at a deeper level.

True friends are those that you know you can count on, no matter what happens to you. Some people in prominent positions think they have many friends, only to find that their friends disappear when they lose their jobs or retire. That's the time when real friends reach out to each other. When Penny was diagnosed with breast cancer, I was amazed how many people supported us.

After Cursillo, I helped form a prayer group with seven friends. Twenty-eight years later we're still meeting weekly at a nearby Minneapolis church. This group has been one of the most meaningful things in my life. Having a group with whom you can share your deepest feelings is a true blessing. We discuss our spiritual and religious beliefs and doubts, career difficulties, marriage and family problems, and the process of personal development.

Each week one member of the group initiates the discussion about an area of his faith or his developmental journey he would like to discuss. Typically, the discussion will be drawn from a reading by authors such as Henri Nouwen, Dietrich Bonhoffer, and Marcus Borg. The discussions are intense but never judgmental. Our faith journeys have led members of the group in different directions, but we come together in a deep sense of mutual caring and respect.

Over the years we have developed a sense of shared history—from having a member with Alzheimer's disease who eventually died to coping with chemical dependency, divorce, challenging sons, death of a child, loss of one's job, and personal health issues. One issue we never stop talking about is our relationship with our fathers, because most of us had complex relationships that we are still trying to understand. My experience in male relationships is that most men are not comfortable talking openly about their vulnerabilities. Being a part of this group has been a great boon to me over the years, enabling me to share more of myself—my weaknesses and my vulnerabilities—with my colleagues at work and to be more authentic as a person.

Twenty years ago Penny and I formed a couples group with three other couples. We have rich discussions at our monthly meetings about our faith, our lives, our families, and our personal growth. We also travel together regularly—for hiking trips in Switzerland and Norway, visiting the Holy Land, or just relaxing together in Colorado.

Mentoring

Mentoring—both being mentored and mentoring others—has led to some of my most treasured relationships and has helped me grow in many new ways. When I was in business school, I had a wonderful mentor who took me under his wing and helped me develop as a leader with real heart and soul, guiding me to understand the deeper purposes of leading in business and society. Dean Leslie Rollins coached me, goaded me, challenged me, and offered me countless opportunities to develop my deeper qualities. He made me furious at times, but it was his penetrating challenges that had the greatest, most long-lasting effects.

One of these challenges in particular is worth noting. Midway through my first year, Rollins asked me to take over the Musser Seminars on "Business and Christian Ethics," which included students from Harvard Divinity School, Episcopal Theological Seminary, and Harvard Business School. Our discussions were wide-ranging and the debates heated, to say the least. I gained a much broader perspective on issues of values and ethics from the divinity school students than I ever could have solely from business school classmates.

Over the years I have had mentors who have been invaluable in guiding my career—Navy Undersecretary Chuck Baird; Admiral Stan Turner; my first boss at Litton, Bob Bruder; and Ed Spencer, the CEO of Honeywell who hired me and gave me so many growth opportunities.

Most people look at mentoring as a senior person counseling a younger person. I see mentoring as a two-way street in which both people learn a great deal from each other. By mentoring many leaders in the next generation, I have been able to walk in their shoes, gain a deeper understanding of what's important to them, understand their work lives and how they are struggling to balance work and home life, and comprehend how they are approaching life. I'm sure I've learned as much from them as they have from me.

At Medtronic mentoring gave me clear insights into what work life is like for younger employees in the company and how they are coping with dual careers and families. Working closely with them also provided creative and original perspectives on our business. My MBA students were especially helpful in articulating the questions young leaders have about the business world.

Community Service

Penny and I have always been active in the community, serving on hospital and arts boards, raising money for the United Way, coaching youth soccer for thirteen years, and reaching out to young people. We have had a number of international students living in our home and even temporarily adopted a homeless Laotian boy until we could move his mother and siblings to Minnesota to their own home. Over the years we have stayed in contact with many of these students, reveling in their growth and being enriched from the association.

There is no doubt that serving your community takes time—time that must come from your work or your family. In spite of the trade-offs involved, community service is an essential part of becoming an authentic leader. It is in working with people of lesser economic means that you get in touch with the lives of diverse people and develop the heart for leadership. Without doing so, it is easy to become isolated in your office and your home, and gradually become insensitive to how difficult life can be for many people.

The Authentic Life: Putting It All Together

Leading an authentic life requires openness to all that life has to offer and a willingness to go with the flow of life. It is important to seek this richness early in life, when you are still in a formative stage and open to the breadth of your experiences. You will be surprised at the way early experiences open up new avenues of exploration for you, lead you to interesting people, and shape your thinking about your professional life as well as your personal life. At the end of the day you will be able to tell your grandchild that you had the courage to dive into life, experienced its joys and sorrows, and left the world a better place.

Part Two

Building an Authentic Company

The next chapters focus on the kind of companies authentic leaders create and how they build them. Not surprisingly, these leaders strive to develop enduring companies just as authentic as they are.

What makes a company authentic? It is guided by a mission and vision and practices a consistent set of values. It empowers its employees to serve customers with innovative products and superior service. The authentic company is characterized by an enduring organization that is disciplined in producing results for all its stakeholders.

These five characteristics of the authentic company parallel closely the five dimensions of the authentic leader:

- *Purpose:* Mission and vision
- *Values:* Company values
- *Heart:* Empowering employees to serve customers
- *Relationships:* Enduring and committed organization
- *Self-Discipline:* Results for all stakeholders

As authentic leaders go about building their companies, an interaction occurs between the leader and the organization that enables each to grow from interacting with the other. Leaders are influenced by their organizations and grow from the experience of shaping them. Through interactions with the organization, they become more effective in their roles. In turn, the organization responds to their leadership. An excellent example of this kind of mutual growth is Lou Gerstner's turnaround of IBM, detailed in *Who Says Elephants Can't Dance?* Gerstner not only restored the IBM organization, the IBM culture influenced his leadership as well.

This process, known as *homology*, gives the organization stability and provides the capacity for internal growth and external success. As a result, such leaders renew themselves and their organizations. Their legacy is a healthy organization that can endure both crises and changes in leadership.

It would be most unusual to have authentic companies not led by genuine leaders. Disingenuous leaders in an authentic company simply will not survive. Eventually, the organization will force them out because their behaviors are inconsistent with the company's purpose and values. This was the case a few years ago at Procter & Gamble and Coca-Cola when the boards of both companies terminated recently appointed CEOs. Having replaced them—with A. G. Lafley and Douglas Daft—both organizations are responding positively and are thriving once again.

Sometimes authentic leaders find themselves trapped in an inauthentic company. At this point, they have two choices: transform the company or get out. And as I found out earlier in my career, transforming an organization is easier said than done. Lou Gerstner at IBM proved it could be done by a CEO, but doing so from a subordinate role is a much more difficult challenge. If authentic leaders stay in an organization that is incompatible with their values but find they cannot change it, the organization will chew them up or co-opt them.

In recent years we have seen many personas running inauthentic companies. They survive in the near term based on their personal power and their ability to work the numbers to produce short-term results. As time goes on, it is inevitable that both the organization and its leaders will experience entropy, the steady disintegration from within. This is why so many CEOs have failed after a few years or led their organizations into decline.

There is a better way to run a company than getting caught up in the short-term game. In the next chapter we will examine how mission-driven companies create greater shareholder value. Then we will explore how authentic leaders create a culture that is both values-centered and performance-driven, how great organizations empower their employees to serve their customers, and how it takes a team at the top, not just a powerful CEO, to build a great organization. Finally, we will look at how authentic companies serve all their stakeholders.

Chapter Four

Missions Motivate, Dollars Don't

The moment one definitely commits oneself, then
   providence moves too.
All sorts of things occur to help that would never
   otherwise have occurred . . .
Whatever you can do or dream you can, begin it.
Boldness has genius, power and magic in it.

                            —*Goethe*

When I joined Medtronic in 1989, the company had a market capitalization of $1.1 billion. I asked a board member what would happen if a raider were to offer our shareholders $2 billion for the company's shares. Reflecting on the shareholder pressures at the time, he said reluctantly, "We would be gone." To which I responded, "Then the board must not believe in the value of the company's future prospects or its basic purpose." Right then, I made a vow to myself to build on the Medtronic mission to create such a valuable company that it could not be taken over.

By focusing on its mission, Medtronic has done enormous good for people in ways that would never have been possible under conglomerate ownership. This has led to much greater value for all its stakeholders—patients, physicians, employees, shareholders, and our communities—and created $60 billion in shareholder value.

Contrary to what the advocates of maximizing short-term shareholder value would have us believe, the best-kept secret in business is that mission-driven companies create far more shareholder value than do financially driven firms. Let's look why this is so.

Valuing the Corporation

It is only through a sense of purpose that companies can realize their potential. It is their raison d'être that animates employees and inspires them to turn purpose into reality. In recent years many companies have "sold out" to the financial community in a never-ending quest to drive their stock price higher. Once a company does so, it is extremely difficult to regain a sense of purpose. These companies eventually get sold off or incorporated into a larger company, or they go into a long-term state of decline. It is a paradox that by focusing on pleasing shareholders they wind up pleasing no one— not their customers, their employees, their communities, and ultimately *not* their shareholders.

The best path to long-term growth in shareholder value comes from having a well-articulated mission that inspires employee commitment. Companies that pursue their mission in a consistent and unrelenting manner will create greater shareholder value than anyone believes possible. The success of such companies as 3M, Wells Fargo, and Walgreen's has been well documented by Jim Collins in his two thoroughly researched books, *Built to Last* and *Good to Great*.

The Essential Ingredient: Employee Motivation

Where do employees fit into the process of creating value? Employees today are seeking meaning in their work. Since they spend more time at work than anywhere else in their lives, shouldn't they demand meaningful work? In mission-driven companies employee motivation comes from believing in the purpose of the work and being part of creating something worthwhile.

With all the focus on meeting quarterly earnings expectations and increasing stock price during the recent economic boom, we have lost sight of the essential role of employee motivation in creating long-term shareholder value. Caught up in the stock market craze of the 1990s, we began to think we could create shareholder value overnight with some immediate top-down actions. Many investors bought this notion and drove up the value of these companies, only to see them collapse not long thereafter.

There are simply no shortcuts to creating long-term shareholder value. Sustainable growth *cannot* be achieved by a series of short-term actions. Real value can only be created by the hard work of dedicated, motivated employees that develop innovative products and services, establish intimate customer relationships, and build organizations over an extended period of time. This is precisely the approach we used at Medtronic that led to a 150 times increase in shareholder value over the last eighteen years. We followed a similar path to that taken for decades by authentic companies like GE, Nestlé, Merck, J&J, Pfizer, and P&G.

The Flaws in Maximizing Shareholder Value

In response to pressure from shareholder groups, many companies have said their primary purpose is to maximize shareholder value. They focus primarily on serving their shareholders, often neglecting their customers. This philosophy is flawed at its core. Companies that devote themselves to maximizing shareholder value will ultimately fail to do so. It is true that a sharp eye to cutting costs can result in significant improvements in a company's short-term position, but unless the cost cuts are followed by much larger long-term investments, the company is bound to lose its way. Shareholder value will stagnate and eventually decline.

Let's dig deeper into why this philosophy is so flawed. In these companies improving near-term shareholder value takes precedence over considerations of marketplace competitiveness and customer satisfaction. Decisions about strategy and tactics hinge on financial considerations. This short-term orientation results in a failure to invest in long-term opportunities. Inevitably, the short-term opportunities to increase shareholder value taper off. At this point top management usually turns to financial restructuring to achieve its financial goals. Nonstrategic acquisitions, divestitures, consolidations, layoffs, and cutbacks generally follow.

By the time these financial moves are completed, the corporation has lost its capacity for growth. Restoring the firm to a growth company at this point is a long, arduous process. Typically, the shareholders will not afford management the time required to do so. Instead, they press for a change in leadership or acquisition by another owner.

As serious as the consequences of a myopic focus on the financials are, they do not represent the most fundamental flaw in this philosophy. The real failing in focusing on short-term value is the inability to motivate large numbers of employees to exceptional performance. Granted, the top people often can be motivated by personal financial gains, but these people represent only a small fraction of the workforce.

For the thousands of people who are designing, manufacturing, and selling products and providing services, maximizing shareholder value has little meaning and provides even less motivation. As a consequence, employees will do their jobs but no more. Without motivation or inspiration of its employees, the company's underlying performance trails off and is no better than its competitors'. Inexorably, this leads to diminished service to customers and mediocrity of products and services. The list of victims of this philosophy is long and growing: ITT, Litton Industries, Polaroid, Sunbeam, Kmart, USX, Westinghouse, to name just a few.

In discussing these issues with middle managers across a wide range of companies, I find there is universal agreement that you cannot inspire employees by urging them to help management get the company's stock price up. They report that typically employees respond with cynicism when they believe management is just using them to enhance its own wealth, not theirs. The excesses of the last decade have reinforced this belief. The data lends justification to this cynicism. While CEO compensation grew ten times in the last decade, real wages of workers remained virtually flat.

The Path to Long-Term Shareholder Value

The authentic way to increase shareholder value is with a mission that inspires employees to create innovative products and provide superior service to customers. Product innovations and superior service translate into increased market share and expanded market opportunities, creating growth in revenues and the ability to sustain price levels. This is the basis for sustained competitive advantage, increased levels of profitability, and higher profit margins. Consistent profit growth forms the basis for sustained increases in shareholder value. This is why the stock market in the past decade has valued companies like Wal-Mart, Microsoft, Intel, General Electric, and Pfizer so highly.

To turn this strategy into a virtuous circle that is self-sustaining, companies must rigorously reinvest a significant portion of their increased profits in R&D, market development, and future growth opportunities, and not let it all go to the bottom line. The success of this approach reinforces the commitment of employees to the company's mission and provides them with ongoing motivation to sustain it. Companies that stay true to their mission through good times and bad can sustain their growth indefinitely. The chart in Figure 4.1 shows how this approach to shareholder value creation works.

Figure 4.1 The Power of a Mission-Driven Organization

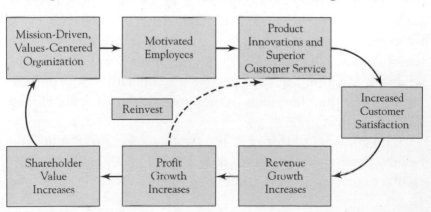

I have witnessed the success of this approach firsthand. When the company consistently provides employees with a sense of meaning and purpose—without deviating and without vacillating—then they will make the commitment to go the extra mile in serving customers. That may mean working well into the night to accelerate the introduction of an important new product, or responding on the weekend to a customer's urgent call for service.

Employees that believe in the purpose of their work are remarkably resilient, even when cutbacks and layoffs are required. This is the experience at Agilent, the leading instruments maker, where CEO Ned Barnholt has done an outstanding job of strengthening employee morale in the face of significant layoffs caused by the recent market downturn.

In my experience motivating employees with a sense of purpose is the only way to deliver innovative products, superior service and unsurpassed quality over the long haul. Competitors will eventually copy any innovative idea for a product or service, but an organization of highly motivated people is very hard to duplicate. The motivation will last if it is deeply rooted in employees' commitment to the intrinsic purpose of their work.

"Alleviate Pain, Restore Health, and Extend Life"

Let's take a deeper look at how a mission-driven company operates, using the experience of Medtronic as an example. In 1962, five years after Medtronic founder Earl Bakken invented the pacemaker, the company was losing lots of money and nearing bankruptcy. It was then that Bakken, with the urging of his board of directors, wrote the Medtronic mission. It gave the company a clear purpose and focus. Within three months the company turned profitable and has been so ever since.

The mission of Medtronic is to restore people to full life and health. This is the heart of the company's success. It has led to spectacular results for patients, career opportunities for employees, and a dramatic rise in Medtronic's shareholder value. It is a hard mission *not* to be attracted to.

The Medtronic mission is reprinted in Figure 4.2. On first reading it, one is tempted to say, "Why is this such a big deal? Doesn't every company have a mission statement?" True, most companies today do have a published mission statement. Typically, it is posted near the CEO's office and reprinted in the company's code of conduct. The difference at Medtronic is that employees really *believe* in the mission and *use* it as a constant guide in their everyday work. It is the mission that provides the inspiration to do superior work with dedication and passion.

Commitment to serving patients has been the principal driver of shareholder value for Medtronic. From 1985 to 2003 Medtronic shareholder value grew at a compound rate of 32 percent a year. This tremendous increase in value has been created not in spite of

Figure 4.2 Medtronic Mission

- To contribute to human welfare by application of biomedical engineering in the research, design, manufacture and sale of instruments or appliances that alleviate pain, restore health, and extend life.
- To direct our growth in the areas of biomedical engineering where we display maximum strength and ability; to gather people and facilities that tend to augment these areas; to continuously build on these areas through education and knowledge assimilation; to avoid participation in areas where we cannot make unique and worthy contributions.
- To strive without reserve for the greatest possible reliability and quality in our products; to be the unsurpassed standard of comparison and to be recognized as a company of dedication, honesty, integrity and service.
- To make a fair profit on current operations to meet our obligations, sustain our growth, and reach our goals.
- To recognize the personal worth of employees by providing an employment framework that allows personal satisfaction in work accomplished, security, advancement opportunity and means to share in the company's success.
- To maintain good citizenship as a company.

commitment to the mission, but *because of* it. As I often said to shareholders at annual meetings and to security analysts, "Medtronic is *not* in business to maximize shareholder value. We *are* in business to maximize value to the patients we serve." This statement is not intended to be a play on words, but rather to acknowledge that long-term shareholder value *only* comes from serving customers.

By engaging the hearts of Medtronic employees, the mission motivates them to create innovative therapies to restore more people, to produce perfect-quality products, and to provide exceptional service. These are the factors that have created customer satisfaction for Medtronic customers and led to significant increases in market share. Medtronic's philosophy really works, and not just in the medical field. It all begins—and ends—with a customer-focused purpose that employees embrace and become passionate about.

Living By the Mission

From the time I joined Medtronic, I was struck by the focus on the company's customers, the patients its serves. In those days the company was restoring three hundred thousand people every year. By the end of 2002 that number had grown to four million people per year . . . one every eight seconds. It's not about the statistics, but the personal life stories. Every person whose life has been transformed by a Medtronic product has a story to tell about the miracle that has occurred in their lives.

The first thing that strikes any visitor to Medtronic is the mission. It is everywhere—in every building, hanging on the walls, and on cards in the wallets, purses, and desks of employees. Next to it are patient photos—people from all walks of life, all ages, and all corners of the globe—all with Medtronic products implanted in them. They look happy and healthy.

Employees discuss the mission constantly—in the halls, the company cafeteria, and conference rooms where life-saving product decisions are made. They share patient stories, talk about telephone calls they receive from patients, challenge each other about whether the quality of Medtronic products is high enough, and dream about new inventions that can restore thousands more to full life. In business meetings leaders regularly refer to it before making important decisions. It is the motivating force empowering employees to achieve extraordinarily high levels of innovation, quality, and customer service.

The Mission-Driven Approach Works for All Companies

Is this approach unique to companies like Medtronic that are in the business of saving lives? Not at all. Many companies offer their employees a real sense of service through their work. Although it may be easier to gain employee commitment to restoring health, any company in any industry can create superior customer service with a purpose its employees embrace.

There are many examples of highly successful mission-driven companies outside health care. 3M employees have been motivated by innovation and creativity throughout the company's history. Intel employees are driven to keep the company on the forefront of technology and to use that technology to serve customers. Microsoft employees are inspired by integrating all the software their users need.

The employees of Target are committed to providing their guests with good value and fashion-forward merchandise in a clean, well-organized store. Goldman Sachs employees have a passion for providing superior service with integrity to their customers over the long-term. American Express Financial Advisors' employees have passion for "providing secure financial futures for their clients."

To illustrate the differences between the mission-driven approach and the focus on maximizing shareholder value, let's examine the recent history of two major banks, Wells Fargo and U.S. Bancorp, both of which have roots in Minnesota. The past ten years, Wells Fargo focused on providing superior customer service, expanding its network of branch banks throughout the Midwest and West. U.S. Bancorp, on the other hand, concentrated on cost cutting and centralizing services. At first, it appeared U.S. Bancorp had the superior strategy; its stock soared when cost cutting led to large profit increases. Eventually, however, its lack of customer focus and problems with employee motivation caused its revenue and earnings growth to stall out. Its stock lost over half its value, leading to the sale of the bank to a smaller Milwaukee banking group. In contrast, Wells Fargo kept its steady growth going, even during the recent recession, and its shareholder value has increased consistently. Today its value is double that of U.S. Bancorp.

Authentic leaders know that *only* by pursuing their missions with passion and commitment can they create sustainable value for their customers, their employees, and their shareholders.

Chapter Five

Values Don't Lie

One of the greatest challenges of businesses today is creating a culture that is both values-centered and performance-driven. Many business executives believe they must make trade-offs between the two. I don't buy it. But doing both simultaneously requires skillful leadership.

Let's look at the question of values before addressing how authentic companies create performance. Values begin with telling the truth, internally and externally. Integrity must run deep in the fabric of an organization's culture. It guides the everyday actions of employees and is central to its business conduct. Transparency is an integral part of integrity. The truth, both successes and failures, must be shared openly with the outside world.

Authentic companies value the importance of stewardship to the people they serve—customers, employees, shareholders, and communities. They measure their success by the extent to which they fulfill the needs and desires of these diverse constituencies.

Authentic companies operate in a democratic and collaborative manner. They are inclusive, welcoming talented people from highly diverse backgrounds and recognizing the strength and stability of differing opinions and diverse life experiences. Such organizations are characterized by a spirit of inquiry, the constant desire to understand the issues in their fullest breadth and to challenge people to develop their full potential—and use it on the job, every day.

The final value of the authentic company is consistency, the steadiness with which the values of integrity, stewardship, collaboration, and inquiry are practiced. Leaders emulate these values in the day-to-day conduct of the business and in personally ensuring their implementation throughout the organization. Values have to be discussed at every opportunity, constantly reinforced, and consistently reflected in the actions of management at all levels.

Articulating an organization's values is straightforward, but gaining alignment of all employees throughout the company is much more difficult. Many leaders believe all they have to do is state their company's values and distribute them to all employees through a code of conduct and their task is done. Then they seem surprised when people's behavior does not conform to their stated values.

Inculcating values throughout an organization starts with the leader, who sets the standard of behavior for everyone in the organization. The leader has to work hard every day to gain alignment with the company's values, reinforcing positive actions and swiftly taking action with employees who do not emulate these values.

Inculcating the Values

One of the most powerful ways of gaining alignment with an organization's values that I have seen is Medtronic's Mission and Medallion ceremony. In this personal meeting with the founder or CEO, new employees hear firsthand about the company's purpose and its values. At the end each new employee is awarded a medallion symbolizing the company's mission.

Shortly after I joined Medtronic, Earl Bakken asked me to come to one of these ceremonies. There I joined thirty other new employees—secretaries, accounting clerks, engineers, and software programmers. Earl started by describing the founding of the company and the invention of the pacemaker. Next he took considerable care to go over every word of the mission. Finally, he invited each of us to come up individually to receive our medallion—a bronze casting with the image of the rising person (symbol of the Medtronic mission) on the front and the first part of the mission on the back. The medallion is symbolic of each employee's introduction to Medtronic, providing a sense of responsibility to carry out the mission.

I still recall Earl's words as he handed me my medallion, "Bill, this medallion is only given to Medtronic employees, not even our customers. Put it on your desk and look at it while you're working. If you get frustrated with your work, remember that you are here to help restore people to full life and health, not just to make money for yourself or the company." I have often thought about these words as we struggled to make our quarterly earnings.

Earl started these ceremonies in the early 1950s when Medtronic had only a few employees. As the company grew, he continued to meet with every new employee of the company as he traveled around the world. One can only imagine the impact of the founder of the company talking with you and asking for your commitment to the mission. Due to Earl's reduced travel schedule in recent years, I took over most of the sessions, and now my successor does them. In 1999, after we had doubled our workforce due to expansion and mergers, I conducted sessions for over eight thousand employees, passing out medallions to each of them.

One of these sessions in particular still sticks in my mind. On my initial visit to Medtronic India, I held the first Mission and Medallion ceremony for our employees there. Throughout the session they were unusually attentive and seemed genuinely moved by the event. Afterward we went from the indoor meeting center to the lawn outside for the Indian tradition of planting a tree commemorating my visit. An Indian healer asked me to sit in front of the tree while he prepared me physically for the ceremony, washing my hands and painting my face with several different colors. Then I had to prepare the ground and the tree itself, while he went through several Hindu rituals with candles, water, and earth. The event took over an hour while all 250 employees stood in a circle around us. I kept watching the employees' eyes to see if they were bored. Not at all. They were watching with rapt attention to see what I thought of *their* ceremony. It was a wonderful, culturally relevant way to share our deepest traditions.

Medtronic has worked hard to preserve the tradition of this ceremony, in the face of a rapidly expanding employee base, now totaling twenty-eight thousand people. It has played an important role in inculcating Medtronic values into the culture. I don't know of any other company of this size that affords *every* employee the opportunity to meet with the founder or CEO to learn about the company's values. Whatever time it takes, it is well worth it.

To solidify Medtronic's values among the leadership team, we created two experiential educational programs to reinforce the values-centered culture. For executives, we initiated the Medtronic Values and Ethics Seminar, modeled after the Aspen Institute's Executive Seminar. Our initial session included executive committee members and spouses and focused on great books and the discussion of modern ethical issues, like universal health care and euthanasia. Based on the program's success, we made it the capstone of Medtronic's education programs for all officers.

One controversial discussion involved President Truman's decision to drop the atomic bomb. Many of the Americans and Europeans expressed the view that the war could have been ended without dropping the bomb. At this point a Japanese participant raised her hand and said, "I disagree completely. Dropping the atomic bomb was exactly what the Japanese people needed to shock us into realizing how wrong our warlike efforts were. After all, just look at what has happened to us in the last fifty years." This story and others are repeated so often around the company that they are part of Medtronic folklore.

Building on the success of this program, we created an educational course for high-talent managers around the world, called "The Medtronic Leader." The program focuses on leadership from the heart and developing the qualities of a leader, applying experiential learning. I participated in all these sessions, sharing my path to leadership and interacting with the group about the leadership issues they face. Enabling people to go inside to learn more about themselves, their strengths and weaknesses, and their impact on others is an important element of their leadership development.

Deviating from Your Values Can Be Costly

When the company's leaders become role models for its values, the impact on the entire organization is tremendous. The trust of the leadership is earned through practicing the company's values every day, not just by espousing them. But when leaders preach one thing and practice another, commitment is quickly lost and employees become doubly cynical.

Without a consistently practiced set of values, employees will not trust the company or believe in its purpose. Leaders may spend a decade in building that trust and lose it all in a single act. Witness the impact on Exxon of the failure of its leadership to respond to Alaskan oil spills after the *Valdez* ran aground.

Recently I used the Enron–Arthur Andersen debacle to make this point with a class of MBA students. I described Arthur Andersen as a tragedy, saying "you can spend fifty years in establishing your reputation and lose it in a day." A Dutch student challenged my characterization, "No, Bill, Andersen didn't lose it all in a day. They sold their soul to their clients over the last five to ten years by compromising their values more and more, just to make money. What looks to you like a giant step in destroying documents was to them just another step in sacrificing values for greed." He was quite correct. What appears to be a compromise of values in a single instance is usually the final act in a series of compromises.

Earlier in my career, I had experienced this firsthand. While I was at Litton, the board of directors visited our microwave oven division to understand the reasons for our exceptional growth record. As I was presenting our worldwide standard of ethics, I noticed the independent directors were nodding in agreement, but the CEO was scowling as though he wished I would move on. At the coffee break I found out why, as I overheard a conversation the CEO was having with the head of the corporation's oil exploration business.

"Charlie, the audit committee is very upset about your audit report," he said. "I know you have to do what you have to do to get the business, but if you ever put it in writing again, you're fired!" The message was clear as a bell: it's okay to make payoffs; just don't get caught. That incident convinced me I working for the wrong company.

Can the Values-Centered Culture Achieve Peak Performance?

One of the greatest challenges for the values-centered culture is to produce top performance and succeed in the market against "win at any cost" competitors. Values are only one part of an organization's culture; the other half is its operating norms—the way in which day-to-day business is conducted. Practicing solid values does not guarantee results unless a passionate commitment to performance standards is incorporated into the organization's norms.

The question is, Do the organization's norms drive performance or do they undermine it? The latter is what I found at Medtronic when I joined the company. The company's long history of success had led to a soft underbelly that manifested itself in a lack of discipline. The company was extremely values-centered, but its internal norms of consensus decision making, conflict avoidance, and lack of personal accountability all undermined the company's performance. For all its strengths, it was my impression that Medtronic's culture was too Minnesota Nice. I realized that these aspects of Medtronic's culture *had* to change if we were going to be an effective competitor and realize our vision of being the global leader in medical technology.

The challenge we faced was changing a successful culture without diminishing its positive attributes. Cultural change is never an easy task, and far more cultural change efforts ultimately fail than succeed. Transforming a healthy culture is even more difficult than changing an unhealthy one. Many people will not understand why change is necessary when the company has been successful. The leader has to be patient, communicative, and diligent in insisting on changes at all levels, or the organization—like the proverbial willow tree—will snap back to its previous mode of operation as soon as the pressure is off.

In Medtronic's case the challenge was especially acute *because* the company had such a positive culture and strong set of values. As the newcomer leading these changes, I recognized that many people in the organization, especially those who had spent their entire careers at Medtronic, would feel uncomfortable with the changes I was proposing. Many of our leaders seemed quite comfortable with the culture just the way it was.

To link the cultural changes to our mission, I framed them in terms of helping patients and winning in the marketplace. In truth, we had no choice but to make the Medtronic culture more performance-oriented if we were going to fulfill our mission. Otherwise, we would lose out to more aggressive competitors and never earn the right to serve those patients.

"It's the Way We've Always Done It . . ."

In addressing the issue of Medtronic's performance standards, I found that goals and deadlines were routinely set, missed, and then simply adjusted. Poor performance was rationalized by excuses. Even incentive payments were adjusted upward to reflect these excuses. As a result, sales targets were missed, new products delayed, expense budgets overrun, all with no direct consequences for the individuals in charge. The organization tended to diffuse responsibility for performance, making it difficult to find out who was responsible. When individuals failed, they were rarely removed from their jobs. Instead, others shielded them from responsibility.

The lack of performance standards related directly to the organization's inability to deal with conflict. Many managers could not abide open conflict in meetings. Disagreements over issues were frequently interpreted as personal attacks. Many people believed it was obligatory that everyone agree before a decision was taken, not just have their point of view heard. As a consequence, decisions were not taken in a timely manner, and conflicts were dealt with indirectly.

To address these issues, we installed a system of closed-loop performance management. In the future, we had to agree on very challenging goals and hold people to their commitments, making schedules, managing within budgets, and achieving sales and profit goals. Surprising as it may seem, this had not been done before. This meant changing attitudes of key people in the organization, raising the performance standards, and replacing those managers who weren't prepared to measure up. This took several years and a number of managerial changes. Eventually, most people realized how important these cultural improvements were to the company's success and embraced them enthusiastically.

Raising the Bar

Medtronic has always had dedicated employees, but the organization often rewarded loyalty instead of performance. Whereas the quality of the first-line employees was exceptional, serious gaps in management capability developed over the years. Many managers were unable to grow at the rate of expansion of the business; their jobs expanded, but their work habits remained the same.

These characteristics, residing deep in the culture, affected customer responsiveness, fiscal discipline, quality of managers, and interpersonal interactions. Unless we changed, Medtronic could not be an effective competitor.

Often growth organizations fail to take a tough-minded approach in assessing their management talent. They limit their future growth by failing to have the depth and breadth of talent required to take advantage of opportunities. Eventually, these organizations lose their competitive edge. A good example is Apple Computer. During the 1980s Apple experienced explosive growth, thanks to the success of the Macintosh computer, but was unable to build its management rapidly enough to keep up. As a result, the company turned to a series of outsiders to fill the ranks of its management, none of whom seemed to understand the computer business or Apple's unique culture. In spite of its ongoing innovations, Apple has never been able to arrest its steady loss of market share.

Creating the Cultural Changes

In transforming Medtronic's culture, we decided not to hire cultural change consultants. Instead, I modeled constructive conflict myself by creating a more challenging atmosphere in our executive meetings. This meant asking probing questions, insisting that managers present each situation in objective terms rather than sugarcoating things with a positive spin designed solely to garner approval. I had learned from my days in the Defense Department during the Vietnam War the perils of well-rehearsed, positive presentations that avoid the essential realities.

My approach led to criticism from some managers. They saw me as too aggressive, too challenging, and too involved in their businesses. After one such session, a senior manager asked, "Is there anything you won't get involved in?" I felt I had to get deep into the businesses to create the necessary changes in behavior. Creating a more challenging environment was natural for me and fit my leadership style. However, it was far less comfortable for managers who were unaccustomed to being questioned.

In those days I talked a great deal about empowerment. One day a mid-level manager confronted me, saying it was not very empowering for me to challenge his plans. Several weeks later he came back to me and said, "Now we understand you better. When you talk about empowerment, you really mean 'empowerment *with* responsibility.'" To which I responded, "Is there any other kind?"

In an organization that has a strong culture and a history of success, the pressure to maintain the existing culture and adopt your predecessor's style can be irresistible. But as Jack Welch recognized when he became CEO of GE, it is often necessary to evolve a successful company's culture to prepare for a more challenging environment. That does not have to be at the expense of its values. As this story illustrates, it is possible to bring your own personality to the leadership post and still be true to the company's history and ideals.

The extraordinary results achieved by Medtronic in the past fifteen years shows that an organization can be both values-centered and performance-driven. The key is aligning the organization's values and performance objectives. Working in complementary fashion, practicing values and driving for performance reinforce each other and enable the creation of a great company.

Chapter Six

It's the Customer, Stupid!

When Louis Gerstner arrived at IBM in 1993 as its new CEO, he found an organization of three hundred thousand employees that had lost touch with its customers. Once famed for its "superior customer service," the mission articulated by Thomas Watson Sr., IBM was so internally focused and political that the meaning of customer service had devolved into servicing machines on customer premises.

I worked for IBM for a summer in the mid-1960s, when the company was the business community's role model for customer service. In those days the motivational speeches were so intense that my first sales meeting felt like a religious rally. Toward the end of the meeting our district manager put up a large map of his territory with a red circle around *every* company that used competitors' computers. Our sales team was dispatched to visit 100 percent of these customers over the next two days and convert them to IBM—now!

The culture Gerstner found in 1993 was the opposite of the one Watson created: customers were viewed as the problem, to be manipulated rather than served. In just three years IBM had gone from the world's second most profitable company, with net income of $6 billion on sales of $69 billion, to an $8 billion loss. The company was losing so much market share to personal computers and hemorrhaging so much cash that many industry experts were predicting it could not survive.

Faced with such a crisis, most "turnaround CEOs" would have reduced the workforce immediately by fifty thousand to a hundred thousand people, chopped the $6 billion R&D budget in half, and started selling off the company in pieces. This is precisely what the security analysts and the media urged IBM's new CEO to do. Gerstner did just the opposite. He kept the company together, reinvested in mainframes, and protected the core R&D budget. To shift the focus back to IBM's customers, he decided to make IBM a market-driven company again—rather than an internally focused, process-driven enterprise—by focusing all initiatives on the customer.

With the company's survival in question, Gerstner also had to make cutbacks in expenses and employment levels. He was able to garner employee support for these painful actions by giving people a renewed sense of purpose, returning to the company's roots of providing superior customer service.

What did Gerstner do to restore IBM's passion for customers? He made himself the role model for customer service. At the company's first customer conference after his appointment (an event that his predecessors never attended at all), Gerstner stayed for the entire two days. As his first step in changing IBM's culture, he announced Operation Bear Hug, insisting that his top fifty executives each visit five of IBM's biggest customers within three months. Most important, he devised IBM's long-term strategy of being an integrator of information systems solutions for its customers.

IBM's steady erosion from a customer-oriented enterprise to an internal bureaucracy is not unique. In fact, its problems are typical of many large U.S. and European corporations over the last fifteen years. As the pressure from shareholders for short-term financial results has mounted, the focus on customers has declined. It's not that the CEO decides to deemphasize customers. Rather, top management's emphasis on internal processes, making quarterly earnings, and endless budget and operational reviews sends a powerful message to the organization that "customers come second."

I witnessed this same phenomenon at Honeywell in the mid-1980s when I was promoted to sector head. To restore the company's external focus and leverage the company's broad capabilities, I organized a cross-corporate initiative on customers. The CEO challenged the amount of time and energy I was spending with customers, saying, "That's the sales department's job." His comments sent me a clear message about what was important.

Much to my surprise, I found similar tendencies at Medtronic when I joined the company in 1989. In its early years the company had been very customer-focused, largely due to the passion of founder Earl Bakken. As the company grew, however, new managers lost sight of the imperative to serve customers personally and wound up spending most of their time in internal meetings. This led to a growing rift between the sales organization and the home office.

Learning Medtronic's Business Firsthand

When I joined Medtronic, I knew a lot about high-technology businesses but virtually nothing about medicine. My predecessor encouraged me to get into the field with physicians to observe implant procedures and let them teach me the business.

It was the best thing I ever did. I not only learned how Medtronic's business works through the eyes of our customers, I got to see the mission play out in hospital operating rooms where the patient's life depends upon the physician's skill and the capability of Medtronic products. I give great credit to Medtronic's physician customers for teaching me about medicine. I never met a physician who wasn't willing to take the time to educate me. All I had to bring was a willing set of ears and eyes and the ability to ask a few leading questions. By spending so much time in hospitals working with doctors, I gained a deep appreciation for the challenges of their work and a real passion for Medtronic's business. The numerous questions I asked internally upon my return from these visits sent the message to Medtronic's executives that they too needed to be in hospitals with physicians and patients.

Medtronic has a highly unusual relationship with its customers. For 70 percent of all Medtronic implants a Medtronic representative is in the operating room, working with the physicians. These representatives are well trained technically and have developed close long-term relationships with the doctors. Many physicians will not start a procedure without the presence of a Medtronic representative.

It didn't take long for my learning process to begin. I saw my first pacemaker implant the second day on the job. The physician used Medtronic's newest pacemaker, one that paced two chambers of the heart. The sales rep was running the Medtronic programmer, giving the doctor regular feedback on whether he had placed the lead in the right spot. The doctor placed the first pacemaker lead easily, but had difficulty with the second. After an hour of struggling with it, he decided it was good enough. The rep objected, saying he was getting marginal electrical contact, but the physician prevailed and sutured up the patient.

At this point the rep took another electrical reading to check the pacemaker. Finding that it fell well short of the minimum required to pace the heart, he insisted the doctor redo the lead. This meant opening up the patient's sutures and spending another hour on the case, neither of which made the physician happy. At this point the rep leaned over to me and whispered, "If I don't insist on doing this over, we'll be back in here in forty-eight hours to redo the patient entirely." After the case was over, he mentioned that this physician implanted only a few dozen pacemakers per year. So I asked, "How many have you done?" "Over three thousand," was his reply.

That one experience taught me a great deal about what makes Medtronic's business go. Our sales reps are the physicians' partners, albeit the junior partners. They carry beepers and are on call twenty-four hours a day, seven days a week, if needed by a customer for an emergency or just a routine question. As the rep told me, "This takes a lot of time, but while I'm with the doctor doing a case, our competitors are on the outside looking in."

This experience was only the first of hundreds of implants and procedures around the world that I observed in those early years. They were a great way to understand the business and to get to know our customers. I came away from these experiences deeply impressed by the dedication of the physicians and their teams and with the caliber of the Medtronic field force.

Not all of these early experiences were positive. I vividly recall an angioplasty case where the doctor was using a Medtronic balloon catheter to open up clogged arteries. The product literally fell apart in the doctor's hands as he was threading it through the patient's arteries. He was so angry that he took the catheter, covered with blood, and threw it at me. I ducked as it went sailing across the room!

After the case the sales rep told me he had seen this happen several times before. He had filed reports on the defects, but heard nothing back. We counted seven organizations his reports had to go through before it got to the people who designed the products in the first place. Something was terribly wrong here. In taking specific issues raised by our customers back to Medtronic's engineers, I found a high level of ignorance and even denial that the problems actually existed. Why? As well intentioned as they were, the engineers were not spending any time with customers and were insulated from product problems. By the time the problems reached them, they had been filtered by many different organizations. The engineers tended to deny the design flaws, often blaming physicians for not using the products correctly.

In meetings with doctors I always asked, "How well is Medtronic serving you?" That first year I got lots of negative feedback about the competitiveness of the product and the lack of openness in dealing with quality problems. I never heard a single complaint about the field sales and technical service organization, which was uniformly characterized as outstanding.

As a result of these early experiences, I decided to make "customer and patient focus" the company's major leadership initiative. My early experiences in the field had a powerful influence in shaping my views on the kind of company we wanted to be: *patient-centric, customer-focused, innovative, unsurpassed in quality and service*. Easily said, but very difficult to achieve.

Customer-Focused Quality

It was evident from these field visits that Medtronic's customers had real questions about the company's responsiveness to their problems and the quality of our products. At the time Medtronic was using the popular Crosby quality program with its emphasis on internal training, testimonial talks from top management, and the concept of "internal customers." All of this was making Medtronic more internally oriented and less focused on its customers. Meanwhile, the quality of Medtronic's products did *not* improve.

We decided to abandon the Crosby program and create our own quality initiative. "Customer Focused Quality" (CFQ) was launched in early 1990 as Medtronic's leadership strategy for the 1990s. This gave it a minimum life of ten years. In fact, it is still going strong, reinforced by the "CFQ Renewal" initiated in 2000. CFQ focused the organization *externally* on customers and used customer feedback as the ultimate measurement of quality. This kept the organization from becoming complacent or arrogant, as our customers could never be fully satisfied.

Recognizing the power of personal observation, we insisted that engineers, scientists, and managers get into hospitals to witness implant procedures. After the CFQ announcement, one engineer came up to me with fire in his eyes and said, "Look, I didn't get a master's degree in E.E. from MIT just to sit around hospitals doing nothing." In response, I asked him how he could design pacemakers without observing implants to see what difficulties physicians were having. This brief exchange brought back memories of my first implant procedure.

We also declared that there was no longer such a thing as an internal customer. The only customers we would acknowledge were the patients, physicians, and hospitals we served. One manufacturing manager told me that he could only relate to the distribution center as his customer. I told him the center was his partner but certainly not his customer.

The Heart of the Matter

In contrast to what shareholder value advocates argue, the purpose of any company boils down to one thing: serving its customers. Ultimately, its success will be measured on how well it serves *all* its customers, especially less powerful ones. If it is superior to everyone else in its field and can sustain this advantage over the long term, it will create the ultimate in shareholder value.

This is true across all industries and all types of businesses: stockbrokers, banks, aerospace companies, consumer goods companies, retailing, high-tech, communications, computers, pharmaceuticals, medical technology, machine tools. Witness the long-term growth of Wal-Mart, Johnson & Johnson, Goldman Sachs, Ritz-Carlton, and Dell, all of whom put primary emphasis on serving their customers.

Top management must be the role model for customer focus, being sure that managers do not slip into an internal orientation. Executives must recognize the employees who are actually serving customers—by creating innovative products and services, by producing quality products, and by providing direct sales and service support—and provide the environment that empowers and rewards their efforts.

A Medtronic district manager who left a vice president's job with a major competitor brought this point home clearly to me. He told me he decided to leave after the company's CEO attacked him publicly at a sales meeting, saying, "Your problem is that you're always thinking about your customers' interests. Your job is to represent the shareholders' interests."

Celebrating the Customer

Achieving and sustaining very high levels of customer service requires continuing focus on aligning employee interests with customer needs. Medtronic has a unique way of gaining employee alignment with its mission of serving patients through an event known as the Holiday Party (which I mentioned briefly in Chapter Two). On this day patients come to the company to meet with employees and to share their stories about how Medtronic products transformed their lives. Six patients. Six life stories. Six miracles. Two thousand employees gathered in a crowded auditorium in a standing-room-only setting. Thousands more watching around the world on videoconference. All eagerly awaiting the stories to come. Earl Bakken, now seventy-nine years old, has presided at this event every year since its inception in 1960. These days he flies in from his home in Hawaii just to be at the event.

A Medtronic executive once told me that all Medtronic employees have "a defining moment" in which they come face to face with a patient whose story deeply touches them. For me that moment came at my first Holiday Party. As I entered the auditorium that day, Bakken suggested I take a careful look at the young person with cerebral palsy who had received a Medtronic drug pump earlier that year. After a few minutes the patients and their families came in, led by a young man named T.J. Flack rolling along in a wheelchair.

T.J. was the last patient to tell his story that day. Abandoning his wheelchair, he walked up the steps to the podium using just his arm braces. T.J. told of the sixteen surgeries he'd had, all in vain attempts to relieve the growing spasticity and rigidity of his cerebral palsy. At age sixteen he had finally had enough and refused further surgery. His body became ever stiffer as the disease progressed. It took him an hour just to get out of bed. Until the Medtronic drug pump transformed his life, T.J.'s simplest acts required Herculean effort. Now he could get out of bed relatively easily and walk up the stairs to his classrooms; even his hampered speech had improved markedly.

As I heard T.J. tell his story that day, my eyes filled with tears. Being new to the company, I felt embarrassed until I glanced at the person next to me. He also had tears in his eyes. It was a galvanizing moment. I saw the mission itself come to life. This one young life crystallized what our work at Medtronic was all about. I realized everything flowed from the mission: restored patients, satisfied physician-partners, empowered and proud employees, and excellent returns to shareholders, enabling us to reinvest in broadening the application of medical technology.

Ironically, Medtronic management had put the drug delivery venture that was responsible for T.J.'s pump on the "divestiture list" the week before I joined the company. After a dozen years of losses, management had given up on the business and decided to spin it off. After hearing T.J.'s story, we went back to the drawing board and looked for ways we could rejuvenate the venture. As a result, we cancelled the divestiture, cut administrative expenses by consolidating it into another business, and invested heavily in R&D and sales. This decision proved to be a good one, as drug delivery became one of Medtronic's fastest-growing businesses.

Infusing Passion for Customers

If we examine organizations that are highly customer-focused, they are usually headed by leaders with real passion for serving the company's customers. Sam Walton of Wal-Mart, Dick Kovacevich of Wells Fargo, Steve Ballmer of Microsoft, Roger Enrico of PepsiCo, John Chambers of Cisco, and Marilyn Nelson of Carlson Companies are just a few of the leaders who come to mind. These leaders set the standards for their organizations to follow, and then create the motivation and incentive systems to reinforce external focus on customers. Serving customers becomes the organization's overarching goal and unleashes the power of employees to use their hearts and their passions to serve.

Chapter Seven

It's Not Just the CEO

One of the great myths of the past decade is that CEOs are primarily responsible for the success of corporations. Rarely is this an accurate picture of how a great company is created. But that's why some boards give their CEOs such outrageous compensation packages and measure them on their ability to get the stock price up. This is an underlying cause of the crisis we face in corporate leadership: as our leaders fall off their pedestals, we lose confidence in the corporations themselves.

There is no doubt that CEOs have tremendous influence on the results of corporations. However, if we examine more closely the great success stories of the past twenty-five years—Intel, Nokia, Hewlett-Packard, Microsoft, Coca-Cola, PepsiCo, just to name a few—we see that each was built by a team at the top, not by a single person. Take Intel, for example. For twenty-five years Intel was led by the triumvirate of Chairman Gordon Moore, Vice Chairman Bob Noyce, and CEO Andy Grove. Together they created one of the greatest technology companies in history. Moore was the visionary of the group, Noyce the technologist, and Grove the person who made it all happen. They engaged in strategic dialogues every day, were comfortable disagreeing with one another, and used their combined capabilities to build a far greater company than any one of them could have built alone.

In *Only the Paranoid Survive*, Grove tells the story of how the three leaders coped with the most difficult crisis in company history. It came as Intel's market share in its core business of computer memory chips was dropping from 70 percent to 3 percent. Checked at every turn by the superior wafer process capabilities of Japanese producers, Moore and Grove asked themselves the hard question, "What would a new chief executive do in this situation?" It was then they realized they had to get out of their original business and devote all their energies to microprocessors, which at the time accounted for only 10 percent of revenues. It was a bold decision, one that enabled Intel to become the world leader in microprocessors and one of the most profitable companies in the world. Would one of them have made that decision alone? Maybe not. It was the clear thinking of the team that enabled them to take such a course.

This example is not unique. Look at David Packard and Bill Hewlett, co-founders of Hewlett-Packard, and the incredible company they built over a thirty-year period. Or the partnership of Bill Gates and Steve Ballmer that has made Microsoft one of the most powerful companies in the world. It has been said—not entirely in jest—that Gates, the software genius and strategist, and Ballmer, the motivator and operator, together are "the best CEO in the world." In the financial services field, Goldman Sachs has flourished as a partnership by creating shared leadership throughout its organization. The combination of John Whitehead and John Weinberg set the standard for investment banking for decades.

On the consumer goods front, the combinations of Roger Enrico and Steve Reinemund at PepsiCo and Roberto Goizeuta and Don Keough at Coca-Cola built two incredibly successful companies. Could they have been as successful operating alone? I doubt it. At least in Coca-Cola's case this was proven. After Goizeuta died suddenly, Douglas Ivester, Keough's successor, was unable to run the company effectively and forced to resign after just two years as CEO.

Great Teams Create Great Companies

As a leader, I have always surrounded myself with people who are more knowledgeable and experienced than I am. The key is having people around you who complement your weaknesses and make up for your lack of experience. This seems obvious, but how many

CEOs fail to do so in building their teams? It is real danger sign when leaders only appoint people with whom they feel comfortable.

Baptism by Fire . . . at Age Twenty-Seven

My first experience in building an executive team came early in my career, when I was thrust into a general manager's role at Litton Microwave at the age of twenty-seven. In my first line assignment, something I had long wanted, I found myself responsible for a division that was supposed to be growing but instead was going downhill.

As I was packing my bags in Cleveland to move to Minneapolis for my new job, I heard the warning on the radio from the U.S. Surgeon General that "microwave ovens may be hazardous to your health." Thus began my long association with the U.S. Food and Drug Administration. A few days later I was in the deputy commissioner's office pleading with him not to pull this exciting new product off the market. They didn't have to. The Surgeon General's warning was sufficient to cause the fledgling consumer sales to collapse and commercial restaurants to post warning signs about possible dangers from Litton's products.

I was not an expert in any aspect of the business, yet in this crisis everyone looked to me for survival. Our first action was to recall the first thousand units we produced and get them up to FDA standards. After that, I spent many long nights at the factory wondering if we could begin production the next day. I survived the crisis only by forming a team with my subordinates, relying on their superior expertise, and prodding them to work together. My skill was to pull together the right people and empower them to solve the problems, one at a time. This is a pattern I have followed throughout my career, as I have lacked substantial industry experience in every leadership job I've had.

To spearhead our launch into the consumer appliance world and compete with the likes of General Electric, Sears, and Whirlpool, I hired two appliance industry veterans who were twice my age and paid them twice my salary. The chairman of Litton had a conniption when he heard what they were making. I stuck to my guns, and he backed down. It was the best money we ever spent.

Somehow we got our act together. Litton became the leader in the consumer microwave oven market with 33 percent share, something we maintained throughout my nine years as general manager. We were Litton's most profitable division—out of 133—in absolute dollars, while increasing sales from $10 million to $180 million and growing the business at an average of 55 percent per year. We never could have done it without such a strong team at the top.

The Executive Office: A Partnership for Leading

My first goal upon joining Medtronic was to create the executive team required to build Medtronic into a great company. The rapid rate of growth we envisioned—doubling at least every five years—could not be achieved through my leadership alone. My initial challenge was to earn the respect and trust of an already established and successful Medtronic management team while asserting my leadership. This is especially difficult when you are surrounded by capable people who have devoted their entire careers to the company. It requires humility about what you don't know, combined with the confidence to use your experience and intuition to make the organization more effective. With my limited knowledge of the medical business, I relied heavily on my new subordinates to educate me, just as I had in my first job at Litton Microwave. Yet I could call upon a wide range of experiences at Honeywell in building high-tech organizations and ensure that we did not repeat the same mistakes.

To build a top quality team around you, it is essential early in your tenure to assess whether you have the people in place who can enable the organization to reach its long-term goals. You should identify the top performers and augment their responsibilities. Those who will not be able to keep up with the growth and expanded job requirements must be moved into lesser roles or retired from the company. If gaps remain, they should be filled as quickly as possible so the team can get used to working together. There may be outliers who cannot accept your leadership, or who are holding back hoping to get your job themselves. It is better that they be replaced early rather than letting them poison the atmosphere. There is no room for politics or dysfunctional competition on a fast-moving, dynamic team.

Shortly after I was elected CEO, I went to Medtronic Vice Chair Glen Nelson and proposed a partnership, rather than the traditional boss-subordinate relationship. We agreed Glen would be involved in all important business decisions, not just those in his area of responsibility, including strategic issues, organization changes, and board matters. Our partnership turned out to be crucial to our decision making.

As a medical doctor, Glen understands the nexus of medicine, technology, and venture capital better than anyone in the entire health care field. I could always turn to Glen with questions about a new technology or medical therapy and get an objective answer. His wisdom and advice were invaluable. He kept me from several poor decisions and encouraged me to remain open to new options, balancing my overly decisive style.

Next I began to think about recruiting a chief operating officer to be my partner on the operating side, someone who could ultimately become my successor. For all of the extraordinary talent we had in Medtronic, I did not see anyone who had the capacity to become COO, much less take over eventually as CEO. With the board's concurrence, we began an outside search.

It didn't take long. Our search consultant immediately proposed Art Collins, the up-and-coming executive at Abbott Labs who was running its $2 billion diagnostics sector. My first meetings with Art went well, as did his interviews with board members. He seemed like the ideal person to be my long-term partner in running the company. We met one night in Chicago and talked about his opportunity to become COO within two years and the leading candidate to succeed me. Something must have clicked, as Art accepted the job two weeks later.

What did I see in Art that made me want to groom him as my successor? From the outset it was evident he had all the qualities required to lead a major corporation. He was smart, articulate, strong-willed, and clear in his thinking. He had a broad perspective on business and health care and, as I learned, exceptionally good judgment about important business decisions. Beyond that, I saw in Art someone who could be a trusted partner during my tenure as CEO. I emphasize the word *trust*. Trust is the vital element that enables two people who work together to know that they can rely on each other implicitly. They know with a high degree of confidence that they are each contributing to the other's success, not just their own.

As the other two members of the Office of the CEO, Art and Glen proved to be terrific partners over the years. They complemented me well, Glen with his keen strategic insights and ability to identify and engage prospective acquisition candidates, and Art with his ability to build quality and depth into Medtronic's operating organization and integrate our numerous acquisitions. We met formally once a week and interacted informally every day. Had it not been for colleagues like Art and Glen, Medtronic could not have accomplished nearly as much during my time as CEO.

The Team at the Top

To mold our top executives into a well-oiled team and bring everyone into agreement on our major goals and objectives, we formed an executive committee that included the leaders of major businesses and corporate staff heads. We met every Monday, operating with a formal agenda published in advance.

Each meeting began with an executive session in which each committee member raised issues they felt needed addressing. We also reviewed and approved all strategies, investments, and financial plans for each business and the company as a whole. I encouraged committee members to make their positions known on areas of the business for which they were *not* responsible. This open approach brought us closer together and built a strong sense of commitment to our mutual agenda. The executive committee actually voted on all major decisions of the corporation, including the release of new products *before* they went to market. This increased commitment to our decisions and emphasized the vital importance of product quality.

Twice a year we held an off-site executive committee meeting. This was a new practice for Medtronic, but a continuation of an approach I had used since the early 1970s. The off-site is an important vehicle for getting team members to express their feelings and frustrations as well as their hopes and dreams. Typically, we employed facilitators so that I could be a full participant. I found this participative approach to executive decisions worked better over time as we built openness and trust and team members got more comfortable with it. They learned they would not be punished for disagreeing with my point of view or anyone else's.

As we were building strength in our top leadership, we still faced two other major organizational problems—a lack of diversity and a lack of organizational depth.

Diversity Isn't About Quotas

A crucial element of a great organization is its diversity, not only in race and gender but also in background and experience. Having people on the executive team who represent a broad range of life's experiences is critical to success. This is not a question of achieving affirmative action quotas but rather of building breadth of thought and opinion into the decision-making processes. Such a team is harder to manage, as inevitably differences of opinion will surface and people want to be fully heard before decisions are taken. It is diversity, and the intense debates it generates, that leads to the best decisions. By calling upon the broad experiences of team members, you can avoid pitfalls and make better decisions.

Throughout most of its history Medtronic has been led predominantly by people with backgrounds similar to my own—white males from the Midwestern United States. Although Medtronic employees came from varied backgrounds, our leaders did not. Our executive team needed more women, more African Americans, more Asians, more people from the East Coast and the West Coast, more non-Americans. Until our leaders reflected the diversity of our workforce and our customer base, Medtronic could not become a truly global organization.

Early in my tenure as CEO we added a very experienced chief financial officer and promoted an exceptional human resources leader. The CFO grew up in an African American family in the inner city of Detroit and achieved great academic and career success before joining Medtronic. Our human resources leader spent the first ten years of her career in the convent learning how to combine humanity with discipline, qualities that greatly benefited her leadership at Medtronic. She had courage to make the tough decisions on people as we "raised the bar" for Medtronic leadership and performance standards. Later additions brought a Zimbabwe native and others with varied life experiences to round out our executive team.

Not everyone saw the benefits to increased diversity. As we were escalating our efforts to broaden Medtronic's leadership, one senior manager came to my office and closed the door. "I thought we had a common goal to make Medtronic more performance-oriented and more competitive," he said. "So I don't understand why you're pushing diversity." I challenged his assumption that diversity would reduce our competitiveness. "In fact, it is just the opposite," I said. "We need to create a more welcoming environment for talented women and people of color or we won't be able to attract the best. This will make us much more competitive over the long run."

It took several years to build a diverse management group, but the payoff in terms of Medtronic's outlook and decision making was tremendous. The perspectives of people with varied life experiences have made the organization more effective in decision making and better able to appreciate its diverse customer base.

Building Organizational Depth

In the 1980s Medtronic had a shortage of organizational depth that had slowed its growth and led to significant quality problems. This problem is typical of high-growth companies that are unable to build their management teams fast enough to keep up with their growth. Growth companies have to upgrade their organizations continuously. This is accomplished through intensive development of internal leaders and recruiting additional talent from outside the company.

My predecessor, Win Wallin, began the organization-building process when he became CEO in 1985. Wallin began with the senior corporate staff, bringing several executives from outside the company, including a new CFO, a new general counsel, Glen Nelson as vice chair, and me. I continued the process, focusing on the business and geographic units. When Art Collins joined Medtronic in 1992, he devoted much of his time to building a stronger and deeper global organization as well as integrating the acquisitions. Anticipating tremendous growth, we put the resources in place in advance of growth spurts so we would be ready when they occurred. It has paid off, as the organization has absorbed rapid expansion and still had the capacity to take on broader challenges.

At first, the organization reacted negatively to the number of outside hires. Although 75 percent of the promotions went to internal candidates, people still worried that the newcomers would limit the opportunities for inside candidates and change the Medtronic culture. As it turned out, the strengthened organization created more opportunities for everyone and the newcomers enthusiastically embraced the Medtronic mission and values. In my view it is essential for growth companies to have a mix of internal and external promotions. Rarely is an organization better off limiting itself to internal promotions.

The strength of the Medtronic organization at all levels and in all areas has been a primary reason for the company's stability, exceptional track record, and consistency. The same can be said for other lasting organizations that continue to lead their industries decade after decade.

Chapter Eight

Whose Bottom Line: Customers or Shareholders?

In the end the success of every leader is measured by the results their organizations achieve for their stakeholders. There is no escaping that reality, regardless of whether you're leading a corporation, a nonprofit, an educational institution, or a government agency. In the end the results produced are the measure of your success as a leader. But the question remains, what results should be measured, and do they accurately reflect the long-term health and viability of the organization?

Stakeholders and the Bottom Line

In recent years the primary measurement of companies and their leaders has shifted to reported performance versus stock market expectations. "Meeting or exceeding quarterly expectations" has the greatest influence on a company's stock price and its short-term shareholder value. The business media are filled with headlines like "XYZ Exceeds Expectations," even if XYZ is reporting a loss. This raises several questions, all of them troubling. First, companies and analysts engage in an interactive game of influencing each other in setting the expectations bar. This has led to inappropriate pressure on predetermining results and increased volatility of stock prices.

Second, stock price is not the best measure because it is so heavily influenced by purchase patterns, investor expectations, market psychology, and the overall trend of the market. It may sound old-fashioned, but I believe the time has come to get back to financial fundamentals as the primary measure. Sustained growth in revenues and earnings per share, cash flow, and return on investment are still the best measures of how well a company is performing.

Third, the telescoping of focus on the short term overlooks the fact the reported numbers are the result of more important measures: how well a company is serving its customers, whether it is gaining market share, how fast its markets are growing, the capability and motivation of its employees, the support it has from suppliers and communities, and its relationship with government bodies. Getting results in these business basics involves a lot more than just managing the bottom line.

Rather than these short-term measures, the criterion for measuring the success of our leaders should be how well they serve everyone that has a vested interest in the success of the enterprise. This is known as the stakeholder model. I was first introduced to it by Henry Schacht, then CEO of Cummins Engine, at a 1970s conference on corporate responsibility. Schacht outlined the stakeholder concept of serving all those who had a stake in the enterprise:

- Customers
- Employees
- Shareholders
- Suppliers
- Communities

I found myself in strong agreement with this approach and began using it in my business—not out of altruism but because it works. Serving all your stakeholders is the best way to produce long-term results and create a growing, prosperous company.

Schacht's predecessor and mentor, J. Irwin Miller, one of the authentic leaders of his era, initiated the stakeholder model. Miller had a keen appreciation of the importance of building a motivated employee base and a thriving community in the company's small hometown of Columbus, Indiana, in order to serve its customers, its suppliers and its shareholders. Although Miller was not widely known outside business circles, his picture once appeared on the cover of *Fortune* magazine during the Watergate era with the caption, "This man should be President," noting that the values and character Miller represented were precisely what America needed in its leaders.

Unfortunately, serving stakeholders has been under attack during the past decade. Since corporate raiders initiated their depredations in the mid-1980s, many financial investors have argued against it. They did so to shift management's focus to generating short-term gains for shareholders, asserting that management's *only* responsibility is to serve its shareholders. Many executives and boards of directors bought into this premise.

For a while the pressure to generate immediate gains had the intended effect. Eventually, the excessive short-term focus backfired, as many companies went into a long-term state of decline and even bankruptcy. Former Sunbeam CEO Albert Dunlap was one of the most vocal opponents of serving stakeholders, stating bluntly, "I don't believe in the stakeholder concept one minute." As if to prove his point, as CEO of Scott Paper, one of the great companies of its field, Dunlap radically downsized the company and then sold it to competitor Kimberly-Clark. His next act was to take over leadership of Sunbeam, the leader in small appliances. It took him only three years to run Sunbeam into the ground and drive it into bankruptcy. After years of shareholder suits, he was forced to give back some of the money he extracted from shareholders in the process.

By focusing solely on generating immediate returns for shareholders, many executives like Dunlap lost sight of the first premise of business: companies can only survive so long as they serve their customers better than their competitors do. They neglected their customers and saw their market shares decline. They broke faith with their employees and wound up with demoralized workforces. They abandoned their suppliers and turned their backs on their communities.

Ironically, in the end shareholders paid a terrible price, as many employees and small investors saw their retirement funds and their life savings collapse, almost overnight. Even conservative index funds experienced an overall decline of 23 percent during 2002 as the result of lost investor confidence in the market. Those who invested in high-flying companies that neglected their stakeholders lost far more.

Let me be very clear about this: there is no conflict between serving all your stakeholders and providing excellent returns for shareholders. In the long term it is impossible to have one without the other. However, serving all these stakeholder groups requires discipline, vision, and committed leadership.

Applying the Stakeholder Model

Look at how the stakeholder model has guided Johnson & Johnson and Merck, two of the most successful companies of the last fifty years. For decades J&J's growth and success has been driven by "The Credo," a clear mission statement that sets forth J&J's responsibilities to serve all its stakeholders. The Credo explicitly lists the stakeholders, beginning with "physicians, nurses, hospitals, and consumers," in the order of responsibility. When Chicago stores sold Tylenol capsules that someone had laced with cyanide, leading to several deaths, J&J CEO James Burke faced the greatest crisis of his career. Burke turned to The Credo as a guide to making the correct moral judgments. J&J not only survived the crisis, it gained great respect for its handling of an extremely difficult problem.

George W. Merck, the son of Merck's founder, told his employees, "We try never to forget that medicine is for the people. It is not for the profits. The profits follow, and if we have remembered that, they have never failed to appear. The better we have remembered it, the larger they have been." Merck's mission states, "our business is preserving and improving human life." It has enabled Merck to be the world's leading drug researcher for decades, and also enabled future generations of leaders such as Roy Vagelos and Ray Gilmartin to address societal problems like river blindness and AIDS in Africa.

The stakeholder model applies across a wide range of industries. At Target, the second-largest retailer in the United States, CEO

Bob Ulrich and his managers refer to Target's customers as "guests" and to employees as "team members." With three hundred thousand employees, many of them part-time workers, Target has a particular challenge to gain alignment around fulfilling its promise to consumers of "Expect More. Pay Less."

Target has instituted a motivation and training program called "Best Company Ever." It inspires employees to be "the best team" members to serve "the best guests," create "the best communities," and thereby produce "the best results" for its shareholders. It works. Target has consistently been the only retailer to compete successfully with Wal-Mart. It differentiates itself by offering fashion forward, price-competitive merchandise in clean, well-organized stores. Without such high levels of motivation from its team members, the company would never be able to make this strategy succeed. Target is also one of the few companies in the world to give 5 percent of its pretax profits to charitable causes across the United States, now exceeding $100 million per year. All of these actions have contributed to Target's 500 percent increase in shareholder value in the seven years since Ulrich became CEO.

Some executives mistakenly believe serving all stakeholders results in trade-offs and compromises shareholder value. As the examples of J&J, Merck, and Target amply demonstrate, the opposite is the case. In serving all the company's stakeholders, the company's sustained success makes shareholders the ultimate beneficiaries.

Part Three

In the Crucible of the Market

Having explored the characteristics of authentic companies and how leaders create them, we turn our attention to the ways in which they achieve success in the marketplace. The market is the ultimate test for authentic leaders and their companies. Can they compete effectively against their most aggressive competitors and establish leadership? Do they generate results that benefit all their stakeholders? And can they remain authentic in the face of extreme competitive pressure in the market and unrelenting pressure from investors to perform every quarter?

When discussing authentic leadership with students and executive groups, I am frequently asked whether winning in the marketplace is consistent with authenticity, even if it means your competitors wind up going out of business. In reality, being a successful competitor in business is at the heart of leadership, just as it is in politics, athletics, academia, and the arts. Leaders must prove every day that their organizations are the best in their chosen field of endeavor, or they will be the next victim of what Joseph Schumpeter labels "creative destruction."

Many people in the business and academic communities believe that missions, values, visions, empowerment, and customer satisfaction represent the "soft side" of business. They see expense reductions, layoffs, divestitures, creative financial management, and write-downs as the "hard side." As you may have deduced, I think nothing could be further from the truth. In my career I have had to lay off thousands of workers, divest failing businesses, take major write-offs, and make large expense cuts. As painful as the consequences of actions like these are, the decision itself is usually obvious and the leader has but few options.

On the other hand, meeting the demanding needs of your customers and motivating thousands of employees toward a common mission and values is much more difficult. So is winning major competitive battles in the market. Authentic leaders know how to deploy their organizations to achieve marketplace leadership and sustain their success for the long term. Because they are so passionate about their cause, they let nothing stand in the way of their success. No one who has ever competed with Sam Walton, Bill Gates, or Andy Grove would ever consider them soft. Yet all three are authentic leaders who have succeeded in sustaining leadership of their markets.

In the chapters that follow, we look at how mission-driven companies overcome barriers to become market leaders, the ways in which ethical dilemmas define their values, how breakthrough innovations illustrate the heart of the company, the use of acquisitions to build and strengthen organizations, and, finally, the difficult trade-offs leaders must make in serving all their stakeholders.

First, let's explore why seemingly successful companies often fail in the end.

Chapter Nine

Seven Deadly Sins

Pitfalls to Growth

Many economists believe companies have a natural life cycle of growth, flattening out, and ultimate decline. But although it is true that many successful companies ultimately do enter into a state of decline, there is nothing natural about it. Their problems can be traced to failures of leadership to preserve the enterprise and sustain its growth. In studying the histories of Polaroid, Digital Equipment, Kmart, Sunbeam, General Foods, Westinghouse, and Control Data, to name some once-great companies that no longer exist, we can trace the mistakes leading to their demise.

The real test of an authentic company is whether it can sustain its growth for an extended period of time without falling prey to short-term pressures or temptations to cut corners. Why is sustainable growth so important? Growing companies attract the most important customers and the most talented employees. Growth provides the funds to reinvest in R&D and market expansion and still increase profits. In the process, all stakeholders can be satisfied simultaneously and growth sustained by reinvesting a significant portion of profit increases.

Pitfalls to Sustainable Growth

Why don't all companies pursue this approach? They fall prey to pitfalls that break their growth cycle and push them into a long-term decline. Let's examine the seven deadly sins growth companies succumb to:

- Working without a clear mission
- Underestimating the core business

- Depending on a single product line
- Failing to spot technology and market changes
- Changing strategy without changing culture
- Going outside core competencies
- Counting on acquisitions for growth

Pitfall #1: Lack of a Clear Mission

The most frequent reason companies get into trouble is trying to grow without a well-understood mission. Without clarity over purpose, it is difficult if not impossible for your customers, your employees, and your shareholders to know what your company stands for and where it is going. Internal decision makers have no framework for making decisions.

International Telephone and Telegraph (ITT) and my former company, Litton Industries, are classic cases of growth companies without a mission. One could say that their purpose was to generate short-term earnings any way they could, regardless of the business they were in or the way in which business was conducted. In the 1960s ITT was the prototype conglomerate, a company that claimed it could grow forever through financial engineering. Its leader, Harold Geneen, acquired the most disparate kinds of businesses, everything from Holsom Bakery to Hartford Insurance. He relied on his own skill and an extremely powerful corporate staff to drive operating heads to produce short-term numbers. Over time ITT lost sight of its birthright as the leading international telephone company, even selling off its telephony business in the 1980s when the company was unable to make the transition from analog to digital technology.

Is it any surprise that ITT no longer exists? In search of ITT's core, Geneen's successor began peeling back the onion that made up the company. He found out, in the words of Gertrude Stein, "there is no there, there." He had no choice but to dismantle the company, breaking it up and selling it off in pieces to preserve some semblance of shareholder value. After the final split, he was left with Sheraton Hotels and some Las Vegas casinos. In the end they too were sold.

For ten years I worked for Litton Industries, another classic conglomerate. Through a series of acquisitions, Litton grew from a single military components business to 133 divisions. There was no corporate strategy, no mission, and no linkage between businesses. As president of its rapidly growing microwave oven division, I had complete autonomy and, like all other division heads, a unique accounting system. Although the top executives were financial experts, they never spent enough time with the operations to realize their monthly financial reports bore little relationship to the business realities.

Eventually, Litton became a victim of its own complexity, and management was forced to sell off many of its parts. Litton Industries itself was sold in 2001 for $5 billion, the same value the company had thirty years before. The lesson we can learn from ITT and Litton is that they had no missions and, eventually, they ceased to exist.

Pitfall #2: Underestimating Your Core Business

There is great danger in underestimating the growth potential of your primary business. In the early 1980s Medtronic concluded that the pacemaker market had stagnated. So management made some extraneous acquisitions that did not pan out while cutting back on pacemaker R&D. Medtronic's share of the worldwide pacemaker market continued to decline, falling all the way from 50 percent to 33 percent. Thanks to a change in leadership, the company divested its unrelated businesses and refocused on pacemakers. The result? Over the last eighteen years Medtronic's pacemaker business grew at twice the market rate, restored its global market share to 50 percent, and achieved double-digit compound growth.

In *Every Business Is a Growth Business*, Ram Charan and Noel Tichy argue that every business can grow if viewed properly and pursued creatively. Jack Welch addressed this problem at GE by demanding that even his most mature sectors expand their market definition to create growth opportunities. He challenged his high-market-share businesses, "How can you redefine your business to take your share from 40 percent to 10 percent?"

Pitfall #3: Depending on a Single Product Line

Many growth companies have ridden a single product line in a growing market to years of rapid expansion. High-tech examples include IBM's mainframe computers, Intel's microprocessors, Nokia's cell phones, and Dell's personal computers. Although all growth markets slow down eventually, often the companies do not see it coming. They are so invested in the success of their core business that they allocate no funds to creating new businesses. When the slowdown occurs, it is too late to broaden their strategy, and they are forced to curtail their investments just to survive.

Cisco Systems is an example of this phenomenon. Cisco grew consistently at 40 percent per year as it rode the expansion of the Internet, dominating the market for Internet routers. When Internet demand collapsed in 2001, so did Cisco's sales. With no other product lines to balance the decline, Cisco was forced to cut back sharply, and its capacity to make acquisitions was capped by an 80 percent drop in its stock price.

Pitfall #4: Failure to Recognize Technology and Market Changes

Many growth companies become wedded to the technology that has led to their success. They miss the emerging technology that will supplant their products because it appears trivial to them, or at least not nearly as sophisticated as their existing technology. Harvard Professor Clay Christianson describes this phenomenon in his landmark book, *The Innovator's Dilemma,* illustrating how "disruptive technologies" take over established markets.

Digital Equipment is the classic example of this phenomenon. Ironically, the genesis of DEC's failure was its enormous success with minicomputers. With its VAX system DEC established the standard of excellence in the computing world, taking huge chunks of share from IBM. When the personal computer appeared on the scene, DEC founder Ken Olson belittled it as "a trivial product." When the PC took over DEC's market, it was too late to respond. Ironically, DEC was eventually sold for a fraction of its earlier value to PC maker Compaq.

Pitfall #5: Changing Strategy Without Changing Culture

Many growth companies, sensing changes in their markets, adapt their strategies to changing market conditions but fail to change their organization's culture. Two classic examples are General Motors and Sears. In response to the energy crisis of the 1970s and the early 1980s, General Motors converted its gas-guzzling V8 engines to energy efficient four- and six-cylinder models. At the same time it dramatically downsized its cars, standardized production processes, and converted from metal to plastics. The result? Its market share dropped from its historical level of 50 percent to less than 30 percent.

What happened? In the process of shifting its strategy, GM did not change its slow-moving culture. It still took GM twice as long as its Japanese competitors did to design and produce a new car. When oil prices headed south and consumers demanded more powerful cars and SUVs, the Japanese and German automobile makers were quick to respond while GM was not. GM cars wound up without the features, styling, or quality its potential customers wanted. The real failure was that the attitude and the culture of GM never really changed, and it was unable to adapt to changing consumer preferences.

The story of Sears is equally sad. Once the world's leading retailer, Sears kept building its infrastructure and overhead in the 1970s as discounters like Kmart began their assault on its market share. When Sears cut prices to match Kmart, it failed to reduce its overhead, and profits plummeted. It was unable to change its culture to the low-overhead, discount mentality, and salespeople continued to use bait-and-switch tactics to get consumers to pay higher prices. Over time its customer base eroded, migrating first to Kmart and then to Wal-Mart and Target. Twenty-five years later, Sears has been unable to reestablish itself as a retail growth company, or to adapt its culture to the realities of today's consumers.

Pitfall #6: Going Outside Your Core Competencies

In the 1960s Honeywell determined its controls business was a slow-growth business. Consequently, the company plunged into information systems, futilely attempting to challenge IBM by acquiring the failing mainframe business of GE. Hard as it tried, Honeywell was unable to gain ground against the market might of IBM.

When I arrived at Honeywell, I did a simple analysis showing IBM's R&D spending exceeded the revenues of Honeywell's whole computer business. Honeywell's strategy of competing across the board with IBM was fundamentally flawed, yet no one was facing that reality. By the late 1980s Honeywell was forced to sell its computer business to its French partner. What went wrong? For all of its expertise in the controls field, Honeywell never understood mainframe computers and got caught in a game where it lacked market power and technological superiority. In searching for growing markets, it expanded too far away from its core competence.

A similar thing happened to Xerox, when it took on IBM in computers to combat IBM's entry into copiers. This was a flawed strategy as Xerox also was unable to compete with IBM. To make matters worse, Xerox neglected its core business, letting Japanese companies take over the low end of the copier market. Today Xerox is recovering from a severe financial crisis, its once-vaunted cash flow having turned to billions in debt.

Pitfall #7: Counting on Acquisitions for Growth

Many companies become dependent on acquisitions for growth, a risky strategy that eventually will fail. A company that relies entirely on acquisitions runs a real danger of making the wrong purchase or paying too much for a new target. If acquisitions are the dominant growth vehicle, operating problems with them will inevitably squeeze out funds required for internal growth.

Until its recent collapse, Tyco was the darling of Wall Street as it grew by leaps and bounds, making more than five hundred acquisitions. Its businesses ranged from medical supplies to security systems, and its market capitalization grew to $120 billion. Then its accounting practices came into question, its stock price declined, and it was unable to continue acquiring. Shareholders lost 80 percent of their value in just one year. Now a new executive team is trying to revive the company.

The same approach led to the demise of WorldCom. CEO Bernie Ebbers built his company through a string of acquisitions, each larger than the last. When the U.S. Justice Department blocked its acquisition of Sprint, WorldCom turned to accounting tricks to offset operating shortfalls. Eventually, it got caught, and its one-time market value of $160 billion collapsed as the company slid into bankruptcy.

Sustaining Growth

Avoiding these seven deadly sins requires disciplined leadership dedicated to sustaining the company's growth. When growth slows, as it inevitably will, leaders have to renew their commitment to growth and seek out new avenues for expansion, avoiding the temptation to retreat into cost-cutting mode. This takes leaders with courage who are prepared to withstand criticism from securities analysts and the media and inspire their organizations to rejuvenate their growth.

Now let's turn our attention to what authentic leaders do when faced with severe challenges in the marketplace.

Chapter Ten

Overcoming Obstacles

Nothing Can Stand in Your Way

> There is a tide in the affairs of men,
> Which, taken at the flood, leads on to fortune . . .
> On such a full sea are we now afloat,
> And we must take the current when it comes,
> Or lose our ventures.
> —*William Shakespeare*, Julius Caesar (*Act IV, Scene 3*)

As they work to convert their missions into reality, authentic companies often confront significant barriers. Many factors—dominant competitors, regulators, patent limitations—can block market access.

Overcoming Barriers

Leaders with a burning passion for their missions have a laserlike focus on overcoming barriers. Bill Gates believed so passionately in Microsoft's mission of unifying computing with an integrated set of software that he was willing to fight the U.S. government with all his might to keep his company from being broken up. Sam Walton was prepared to take on the dominance of both Kmart and Sears to turn Wal-Mart into the world's leading retailer.

The leader must get everyone working together toward fulfilling the company's mission. This requires two things, strategic focus and a burning desire to succeed. Strategic focus means identifying what's required to fulfill the mission and then making it happen. The organization must be totally committed to doing what it takes to become the market leader. This kind of commitment requires long hours and an unrelenting desire to win. Anything less ultimately will not succeed.

When Jorma Ollila became CEO of Nokia in 1992 at age forty-one, he inherited an unfocused conglomerate. Ollila had the courage to shed 90 percent of Nokia's businesses and bet everything on mobile communications and telephony. He was so passionate about his company's mission of becoming the global leader in mobile phones that he engaged his engineers to write the Nordic digital standards and got them accepted as the European standard. The new standards gave Nokia a competitive advantage that it leveraged into global leadership by 1998.

When the dominance of Japanese producers forced Intel to exit the computer memory chip business, Andy Grove and Chairman Gordon Moore gambled everything on Intel's microprocessor technology. They embarked on a long, hard struggle to gain leadership over many rivals, including market leader Motorola. When Motorola took the early lead by contracting with Apple for all its personal computers, Intel countered by selling IBM its 286 microprocessor and agreeing to license several competitors without royalties. Grove launched "Project Crush" to focus his organization on winning accounts over Motorola. When Intel introduced its next-generation 386 microprocessor, IBM decided against using Intel, preferring its in-house version. So Intel countered by contracting with Compaq and all the other emerging players and eventually wound up with the lion's share of the market.

Two generations later, Intel took the bold step of insisting its customers label their PCs with Intel's new slogan, "Intel Inside." While this move did not please its immediate customers, Intel was able to establish itself as the premier microprocessor company in the minds of end users. Today its market share exceeds 80 percent. Grove's overarching commitment to make Intel's technology the industry standard enabled his company to become the market leader.

Sometimes regulatory hurdles block market access. Swiss biotech company Serono faced just this problem in getting its multiple sclerosis (MS) drug Rebif into the U.S. market. Rival Biogen had been granted an "orphan drug" exclusive by the U.S. FDA for its MS drug. So—in an expensive randomized trial—Serono adopted the high-risk strategy of proving Rebif's *superiority* instead of the traditional approach of demonstrating equivalency. When clinical results proved Rebif's superiority, Serono was granted FDA approval. As a result, Rebif has become the leader in the U.S. market, and Serono just surpassed Biogen to become the world's second-largest biotech company.

Gaining Market Access

When Win Wallin became CEO of Medtronic, he too faced seemingly insurmountable barriers to gaining entry into the implantable defibrillator market. What Wallin understood better than anyone else in the industry was that Medtronic had to be the leader in the defibrillator market, or its core pacemaker business was in jeopardy. The defibrillator represented more than just the fastest-growing product in medical technology. It was key to protecting Medtronic's pacemaker franchise from a major competitor like Eli Lilly that had strong positions in both fields.

Shortly after Wallin arrived, Lilly obtained a court ruling that Medtronic had violated its patents, and Medtronic had to shut down its research as well as marketing efforts. This decision put Medtronic's entire mission at risk. Unless it could gain market access, there was no way Medtronic could get its superior life-saving technology to patients that desperately needed it.

A Creative Inventor Spurned

Ultimately, the defibrillator proved to be the most important medical product of the decade and drove Medtronic's growth throughout the 1990s as Medtronic went from no share at all to more than 50 percent of the world market. Let's take a closer look at what it took to get Medtronic's life-saving products to market.

The story begins back in 1970 when Medtronic founder Earl Bakken attended a pioneering lecture by Dr. Michel Mirowski on his invention of the implantable defibrillator. Shortly thereafter, Mirowski and Bakken agreed on a joint development program and signed a licensing agreement granting Medtronic exclusive rights to the defibrillator. The joint development encountered problems from the outset. While Mirowski and his team were passionate about the product and eager to get it to human clinical trials, Medtronic's engineers found the design's technical problems overwhelming.

Eventually, Medtronic management concluded that the implantable defibrillator was twenty years away from commercial viability and disengaged from Mirowski and his team. Although Medtronic's assessment proved correct, Mirowski took Medtronic's decision as a personal affront. Medtronic's rejection just drove him harder to prove it worked.

The divorce did not go well. Medtronic and Mirowski sued each other over patent rights in a series of court battles lasting seven years. To settle the matter, Medtronic eventually paid Mirowski to go away, thereby giving up all rights to his patents. It was a costly decision; Medtronic was unable to enter the implantable defibrillator market until 1993, taking the case to the U.S. Supreme Court just to earn the right to develop its own product. The total bill: $100 million.

The same year Wallin took over Medtronic, pharmaceutical giant Eli Lilly acquired Mirowski's defibrillator, and months later the FDA granted approval for U.S. marketing. Wallin immediately mounted an aggressive R&D and legal effort to get into the business, giving his R&D team an unlimited budget and the mandate to get a product to market as quickly as possible. Medtronic's engineers decided to leapfrog the Lilly defibrillator with a revolutionary design. With Lilly's entrenched monopoly, they knew that matching the Lilly design would be insufficient to gain market leadership. The Medtronic design took longer to get to market, entailed greater risk, and required a more challenging route to FDA approval, but was essential to long-term success.

A Trip to the Supreme Court

Just as Medtronic's development efforts were heating up, so were the legal issues. To maintain its monopoly, Lilly used Mirowski's patents to keep Medtronic off the market as long as possible. In 1988 a Philadelphia judge gave Lilly a big victory, prohibiting Medtronic from further research as well as assessing $26 million in damages.

Never someone to back away from a fight, Wallin took on the battle with a vengeance. He immediately took the case to the U.S. Court of Appeals and countersued Lilly for violating Medtronic's pacemaker patents. Then he told his engineers to pack up and move the defibrillator project to Medtronic's Dutch R&D center, where Lilly's U.S. patents had no jurisdiction.

Medtronic got its first break when the Court of Appeals reversed the earlier decision, causing Lilly to appeal the case to the U.S. Supreme Court. Ron Lund, Medtronic's new general counsel, believed that the case in the Supreme Court would turn on the language of the law more than on patent issues. To present Medtronic's case, he selected Harvard law professor Arthur Miller. Widely known for his television show, *Miller's Court*, Miller had a wealth of experience in arguing cases and significant standing with the Supreme Court justices, but little experience in patent cases.

February 1990: The air was buzzing with excitement in the Supreme Court the day of the case. The courtroom was filled with executives and attorneys as well as Wall Street analysts. We watched as the nine justices made logical mincemeat of the attorneys in a criminal case. When the time came to present Medtronic's position, Miller stood in the semicircular pit in front of the justices. No sooner had he begun than the justices started quizzing him from all sides.

At the crucial point Justice Antonio Scalia leaned forward over his desk, his heavy black eyebrows moving up and down with an intensity that matched his intellect. Scalia launched a severe challenge of Miller and his interpretation of the law, asking him four consecutive questions in rapid-fire fashion. Anticipating Scalia's reasoning at every turn, Miller offered a clear, logical explanation in response to each query. After the last, Justice Scalia nodded and sat back in his chair.

The remainder of the case was anticlimactic. Miller responded crisply to every challenge before ceding the pit to the opposition. Ever the master of his audience, Miller reminded me of Sir Laurence Olivier playing Hamlet. The Lilly attorneys did a workmanlike job of presenting their case, but in no way could they compare with Miller. Four months later the Supreme Court announced a 6–2 decision in favor of Medtronic. Justice Scalia wrote the majority opinion.

A Landmark Agreement

Medtronic's victory celebration did not last long. We were still confronted with a whole raft of additional Lilly patents on its defibrillator, any one of which could block our entry into the defibrillator market for a decade. Meanwhile, we proceeded with our case against Lilly on pacemaker patents. That fall we heard through a Lilly executive that its new CEO was willing to discuss settlement options.

In our initial meeting Lilly's CEO said he was open to a royalty-free cross-license covering all defibrillator and pacemaker patents. In exchange, he insisted that Medtronic make an older version of our pacemakers for Lilly, as its current products were not competitive in the market. Internally, some Medtronic executives opposed making pacemakers for Lilly because they feared that this would enable them to regain their position in this market. Eventually, we decided that gaining assured access to the defibrillator market was far more important. After six months of negotiating, we signed the landmark cross-license agreement with Lilly. We could enter the defibrillator market as soon as FDA approval was received.

This long battle illustrates the importance of tenacity and focus, two qualities that Win Wallin has in abundance. A less aggressive leader might have blinked in the face of Lilly's legal prowess, but Wallin persisted in his drive to win this essential contest.

Not So Fast! The Challenges of FDA Approval

One battle down—another just beginning: little did any of us suspect the challenges ahead to get FDA approval, the last hurdle before Medtronic defibrillators could be marketed.

We submitted our formal approval request to the FDA in the fall of 1990, shortly before Dr. David Kessler was appointed its new commissioner. A year later the FDA's physician advisory panel unanimously recommended approval of Medtronic's defibrillator. Normally, this leads to final FDA approval in two to three months, but instead everything ground to a halt. Medtronic's regulatory team could not even get the FDA staff to take a telephone call; Kessler banned all telephone conversations with manufacturers. We were completely in the dark as to the status of this vital life-saving product.

Later we learned that Kessler, dissatisfied by the scientific rigor of medical device reviews, had assigned a team of his top drug scientists to examine the review process. They chose Medtronic's defibrillator application for examination against the drug standard. These scientists believed medical devices should have randomized trials using a placebo—a sugar pill—just as drugs did. At this point we became concerned that our product might be held up indefinitely.

Weeks and months drifted by with no feedback from the FDA. Finally, a year later, there was some light at the end of the tunnel when we received an "approvable letter" from the FDA listing minor changes required for approval. We thought we were home free. So did the stock market as the news drove Medtronic stock up 30 percent. We were wrong again.

Once more the telephone lines from the FDA went silent. With our frustration rising, we kept pressure on the FDA from every conceivable angle: U.S. Senators, Congressmen and their staffs, leading physicians who conducted the clinical trials, and the media. Finally, in February 1993, two and a half years after our submission and eleven years after Medtronic began developing the defibrillator, the FDA letter approving the Medtronic defibrillator came. A big cheer went up inside the company. We were finally launched!

And Now—To Market

Within three months Medtronic captured 30 percent of the market, while Lilly's share declined to 50 percent. But the race was just beginning, as both companies had major technological advancements in clinical trials. Eighteen months later Medtronic received FDA approval for a revolutionary new defibrillator that was so small that physicians could implant it in the pectoral region just like a pacemaker, rather than having to surgically open the patient's abdomen. In just two months Medtronic gained twenty points of market share, to 50 percent, taking over market leadership from Lilly for the first time. The following year Lilly divested its medical device divisions, creating a new company called Guidant.

Losing the Lead

In the high-tech business you can never feel secure being the market leader. Not to be outdone by Medtronic, Guidant successfully changed the rules of the game with a new dual-chamber defibrillator that paced two chambers of the heart. Medtronic's first reaction was to dismiss the device as large and clunky with marginal therapeutic benefits. We were wrong: physicians flocked to Guidant, preferring the dual-chamber approach to Medtronic's smaller device.

Fortunately, Medtronic's engineers had another revolutionary design in the works, one that would prevent unnecessary shocks, providing a competitive advantage over Guidant. Only time was against us. Guidant's incremental design got it to market sooner, without an elongated FDA approval process. Medtronic's choice of an entirely new design meant that it would take us a full year longer to get to market, leaving Guidant alone in the dual-chamber segment of the market. Once again, we were behind the eight ball:

Guidant retook the market lead with 50 percent share, while Medtronic's share dropped to 35 percent.

. . . and Battling Back

As the person responsible for the company, I received a lot of criticism from Wall Street for letting Guidant retake the lead. The securities analysts were challenging our research program and our product development capability, and even suggesting that the FDA was taking retribution against us. None of these things was true. Fortunately, this time around the FDA was working *with* us and granted approval of our new design in less than four months.

Eager to regain lost share, Medtronic's powerful field organization took off like a rocket when the approval was received. Within six months Medtronic regained market leadership, restoring our share to 50 percent. For the first time in the fifteen-year battle for the defibrillator market, Medtronic held a sustainable lead over Guidant. For the past four years Medtronic's market share has stayed above half of the market.

Winning this battle was a long, hard struggle, but the prize has been worth every ounce of effort. The intense competition and rapid innovation on the part of able competitors drove technology development at a rapid rate, thereby providing patients with vastly superior products. To overcome the many barriers to market leadership, it takes leadership committed with passion for its mission, with a singular focus and commitment to succeed.

Chapter Eleven

Ethical Dilemmas

When in Rome, Don't Follow the Romans

Many leaders believe ethics is a topic that is discussed in business schools but not a part of everyday business. In fact, ethical dilemmas and pitfalls surround most significant decisions that a business leader makes. Sometimes these issues are moral, sometimes legal, and sometimes personal. Often the most significant challenge in dealing with ethical dilemmas is recognizing them to begin with and then confronting them in business decisions.

Most companies have clear statements of values and ethical codes of conduct that their employees must sign. In spite of these declarations, neither the organization's nor its leaders' ethical practices are established until they are tested under difficult conditions in the market. How leaders respond to these challenges, as painful as they may be, sets the ethical tone for the entire organization and establishes the company's true values, much more than written statements, compliance documents, and training sessions.

Confronting a Public Crisis

Sometimes excellent companies fail to respond to an ethical crisis because they do not grasp its depth or severity, or their leaders choose not to get personally involved. When failures of Firestone tires led to several deaths of people driving the Ford Explorer, the leaders of the two companies chose to blame each other rather than addressing the loss of human life. When the *Exxon Valdez* ran aground off the coast of Alaska, causing a major oil spill that killed millions of fish and literally wiped out the livelihood of hundreds of fisherman, Exxon's top management isolated itself in its New York offices and failed to go the scene of the problem. Later a jury assessed $5 billion in damages against Exxon, in part due to its lack of sensitivity to the impact of the tragedy. Even a great company like Intel was slow to recognize its users' reactions to the flaw in the Pentium chip. Once it did, however, Intel's positive response preserved its reputation.

For a classic case study of how to handle these kinds of crises, look at how the leadership of James Burke, then-CEO of Johnson & Johnson, enabled his company to respond quickly and responsibly to the deaths of several people that ensued when someone tampered with Tylenol on store shelves, adding cyanide to some of the capsules. Although J&J bore no responsibility for the incidents, Burke's very open public response to pull all the product off the market until new packaging could be designed not only saved the brand, it wound up enhancing J&J's reputation as a responsible company.

An Ethical Challenge in Europe

To my surprise, I faced a severe values test during my first year with Medtronic. As part of my first reorganization, I appointed a new president of Medtronic Europe, who had previously been president of Medtronic's Dutch pacemaker subsidiary.

Shortly after taking over, he proposed the acquisition of the subsidiary's Italian distributor. The price for the business was very high, but he insisted we had to buy it or risk losing the business. During due diligence, Medtronic's auditors uncovered inappropriate accounting for a sham contract for Italian marketing services. When the controller was asked what the account was for, he refused to answer, saying that it was integral to doing business in Italy.

After General Counsel Ron Lund brought the issue to me, we hired a special legal investigator. His preliminary report indicated that the funds were traced to a secret Swiss bank account set up on behalf of the Italian distributor. There the trail stopped. Although he could not prove it, the investigator believed the funds were being used to pay off Italian physicians. At this point we informed the Medtronic board and asked them to set up a special committee to oversee the investigation.

I called our European president and told him to come to Minneapolis immediately. When asked about the promotion account, he replied, "You don't want to know about that fund." I told him that indeed we did. At this point he got very defensive, even hostile, saying, "That's the trouble with you Americans. You're always trying to impose your values on Europeans. Business is done differently in Europe." Finally, I said, "These are not American values. They are Medtronic values that apply worldwide. You violated them, and you must resign immediately."

At this point we notified all concerned government bodies of our findings. We also put out a press release disclosing them and making it clear that these actions were completely contrary to Medtronic policy. The announcements caused an upheaval among the employees of the Dutch subsidiary. Many felt the terminations were a political action by Medtronic management designed to eliminate their autonomy. After a few weeks, however, things settled down. For the last twelve years the subsidiary has been an outstanding performer.

This affair was difficult for me to handle because I had appointed the new European president. I had to acknowledge that I made a huge mistake in not checking out his values *beforehand*. Correcting someone else's mistakes is a lot easier than facing your own. It is then that you have to look yourself in the mirror and recognize that you blew it, not someone else.

A Crisis in Japan

The following year we faced a second major crisis, this one on the opposite side of the world. One day Lund came to my office to inform me that two Medtronic-Japan managers had been arrested and put in jail. As the story unfolded, we learned that they had given airplane tickets to a physician so that he could give two speeches at international transplant conferences.

We knew that there had been an investigation going on, but were unaware that any actions were imminent. Art Collins immediately contacted the president of Medtronic-Japan in Hong Kong and told him to get back to Tokyo to address the problem. Two days later he left a voice mail saying, "Everything is under control."

Everything was definitely *not* under control. Collins and Lund got on the first plane for Tokyo. When they arrived, there was a funereal scene in the Medtronic offices. Everyone was paralyzed with fear that they might be the next to be arrested. Lund found that Medtronic's attorneys had advised us "not to worry" prior to the arrests. He immediately changed lawyers, engaging one of Tokyo's top firms.

The new lawyers gave a grave report on the situation, noting that the arrests resulted from an investigation by the Ministry of Health and that Japanese employees of other foreign pacemaker manufacturers had already been charged with wrongdoing. They also learned that the Ministry was very concerned about pacemaker prices and upset with the industry for not agreeing to voluntary price rollbacks.

In late December we were informed that the two sales managers would be released from jail if they would plead guilty. We believed they had not done anything wrong and their actions were well within acceptable marketing practices in Japan. Reluctantly, we agreed to the terms, and the employees returned to their jobs.

Now it was my turn to go to Japan and express apologies on behalf of the company for any embarrassment our actions had caused the Ministry. In addition to meeting with employees in Medtronic-Japan, I had a dozen meetings with a variety of officers at the Ministry of Health. All the meetings got around to the question whether we would agree to reduce our prices. We did not back down, explaining that our prices were fair and consistent with pricing in the Japanese market.

After that, Medtronic took the lead with medical device manufacturers in establishing an industry-wide code of conduct that was later approved by the Ministry of Health. Ten years later there have been no repeat incidents. Prices are still negotiated every two years with satisfactory outcomes, and Medtronic maintains excellent relationships with the Ministry of Health.

This incident taught us the importance of understanding the standards of every local government where the company does business, and the importance of the local environment in judging marketing practices. Although we believed we were operating appropriately, we failed in communications with the local ministry to hear its feedback and respond accordingly. Doing so throughout the world requires local people who are sensitive to the broader policy issues as well as corporate staff that provides the link to corporate policy.

When in Rome?
Ethical Dilemmas and Global Standards

As a student at Harvard Business School, I got into heated debates with classmates about whether U.S. ethical standards should be applied internationally. In the cases we studied it was clear that many non-U.S. companies used a different set of ethical standards in doing business around the globe. So did some U.S. companies. We referred to this as, "When in Rome, do as the Romans do." In these debates I was a vigorous proponent of a common worldwide ethical standard, arguing that a company would lose business in certain cases but also gain from having a clean reputation. Looking back, I realize my views haven't really changed.

One thing that has strengthened my advocacy for a single worldwide standard of ethics is the global nature of business today. Your company's reputation for integrity, or the lack thereof, travels with you wherever you do business. Having a clear set of standards is easier for international employees to follow than is a flexible standard that adapts to local market conditions. With ultimate responsibility for the actions of employees throughout the world, leaders can sleep a lot better if they know that employees are adhering to a common ethical standard.

Nevertheless, temptations to stretch the rules to meet competitive practices are always there, especially in the developing countries. We learned the hard way that upholding an ethical standard takes a lot more than written statements and clear verbal messages. It requires a detailed system of compliance, enforcement, and punishment for improper action. To make such a system work, employees need to be trained on the standards, using real-world examples. Otherwise, there will be misunderstandings or rationalizations about what is acceptable practice.

The key is having open lines of communication with people on the firing line at the country level. They need to know that top management will support them when they adhere to the standard and lose a contract or a customer. There also has to be a vehicle such as a hot line for employees to inform management confidentially of deviations without fear of retribution.

When I arrived at Medtronic, I assumed the company's values of integrity and honesty meant that international management adhered to similarly high standards. So I was unprepared for the business conduct problems we encountered early in my tenure. Confronted with these problems, we took an aggressive, proactive approach and got them corrected permanently. It took several years to get 100 percent compliance with our standards for business conduct. These efforts enhanced Medtronic's reputation around the world and made it easier, not harder, to do business and gain share.

In retrospect, these ethical problems provided an excellent opportunity to establish clear standards for employees throughout the world. Addressing them before Medtronic's growth spurt allowed us to expand Medtronic's global operations with the confidence that the business being generated was sound and all employees were on the same page in terms of ethical standards.

Chapter Twelve

Innovations from the Heart

In college I studied industrial engineering. On summer jobs I used a stopwatch to do time and motion studies of the processes used by machine tool workers. In those days the emphasis was on maximizing the efficient use of people's hands. In the past twenty years we have shifted emphasis to the "knowledge worker," aiming to make full use of people's brains. Even production workers at Medtronic became knowledge workers as they did their own quality control, ran their personal computers, and helped solve product problems.

In the twenty-first century great companies will figure out how to tap into people's hearts—their passions and their desires to make a difference through their work. They will do so by appealing to their employees to fulfill the company's mission through continuous innovation and superior customer service. It is the passion and spirit that come from the heart that has enabled companies like Procter & Gamble, Dell, Microsoft, 3M, and J&J to sustain their growth in spite of economic downturns, operating problems, and changes in top management.

Passion Begets Innovation

As organizations get larger, the natural tendency of managers is to control the business with rules, processes, and procedures. A growing bureaucracy is a huge barrier to innovative ideas and dampens creativity, no matter how much it spends in research and development. Leaders committed to innovation have to work hard to offset these tendencies, giving preference to the mavericks and the innovators and protecting new business ventures while they are in the fragile, formative stage.

To do so, effective leaders must stay close to the innovators that create organic growth. This means walking through the labs and learning about creative ideas before they get killed off by middle management in the budget-cutting process. Founder Bill Hewlett made "management by wandering around" an integral part of Hewlett-Packard's culture. 3M has long had a leadership culture that won't let creative ideas die or get squeezed out.

Leaders are also in the marketplace continually looking for innovative ideas and bringing them back to the company's creative people. Medtronic founder Earl Bakken and, more recently, Vice Chair Glen Nelson have been masters at getting to leading-edge physicians, understanding their creative ideas, and working with them to create the innovative designs that convert their ideas into products. This has been the backbone of Medtronic innovations.

Companies that link the passions of their employees to the generation of innovative ideas will have the capacity to sustain their growth for decades. Growth itself creates a virtuous circle that motivates employees through its success and provides funds to sustain expansion. Doing so requires the development of multiple growth vehicles, time-phased over the near, intermediate, and long term, and funding them consistently. When one growth market tapers off, the next growth vehicle must be prepared to take hold and drive the company. This requires skillful and dynamic planning from the top executives.

Near-term growth vehicles provide the immediate earnings growth to sustain the business and the funds flow for investment in higher-risk growth opportunities. Leaders must know with a high degree of certainty which businesses will provide this immediate growth, and whether they will be sufficient to offset slower-growth or declining businesses. Intermediate growth vehicles—those that come on stream in the two- to five-year time frame—should also have a high probability of becoming reality on a predictable timetable.

Long-term growth vehicles, those that pay off in five to ten years, contain an inherently high degree of risk and uncertain timing, but their market potential can be enormous. Because of the uncertainties, it is essential for the growth company to invest in many such vehicles, as most of them will not materialize. The danger comes when management gets discouraged too soon with their progress and cuts back funding. This can be a very high risk if the company is missing its near-term goals.

The Story of Gleevec

To illustrate the power of innovation to transform a company, let's look at the story of Novartis's development of Gleevec, one of the most important new drugs in the pharmaceutical industry. Gleevec is the first of a new class of compounds directly targeting the disease, in its case a cancer called chronic myeloid leukemia (CML). Just a couple of years ago Gleevec was languishing in the Novartis labs when it was "discovered" by CEO Dan Vasella. Although the Novartis marketing staff had the drug on the back burner because of the small number of CML patients, as a medical doctor, Vasella recognized the drug's potential. Overcoming some internal resistance, he accelerated clinical trials for Gleevec. The results were so astounding that the FDA approved the drug in record time. Today Gleevec is enhancing the company's reputation on its way to become another Novartis "blockbuster" and is inspiring breakthrough innovations throughout the company. Vasella is leveraging its success to expand dramatically the company's R&D spending.

Vasella introduced the drug in a most creative way. Recognizing that the drug's cost would cause a hardship for lower-income people, he announced that Novartis would provide the drug for free for anyone with an income of less than $40,000—and at a reduced cost for patients with incomes up to $100,000. In a time of concern over pharmaceutical costs, the Novartis initiative was especially well received by the U.S. Secretary of Health and Human Services.

Gleevec has had a most positive impact on Novartis's reputation in the United States, far exceeding its initial sales. It illustrates the power of an innovative idea and the heart that Vasella and Novartis have for their patients.

"Reinventing Medtronic"

Medtronic's strategy for innovation has enabled the company to sustain an 18 percent compound growth rate over the past eighteen years. These dramatic examples of Medtronic innovation reveal the "heart" of Medtronic and illustrate why employees are so motivated to create them.

Medtronic's high-growth era began in 1985 when my predecessor set a 15 percent growth goal, requiring the company to double every five years. At the time Medtronic had only $400 million in revenues, so doubling the business was quite realistic. These days Medtronic must add $7.7 billion in annual revenues every five years to grow at 15 percent, requiring it to invest in larger markets with higher payback.

Medtronic publicly announced the 15 percent growth goal to shareholders, employees, and customers. We maintained this goal even in years when our growth either slowed or soared well above 15 percent. Setting a public growth goal is an outstanding discipline for the entire organization, one that forces management to make the strategic investments to keep growth going.

There have been several times over the years when senior executives argued that the goal should be lowered to match the realities of slower-growth markets. As CEO, I steadfastly resisted any attempts to change it because I felt it was essential to Medtronic's continuing success. When faced with shortfalls, I found the 15 percent goal became an important discipline that forced us to search harder for new avenues for growth.

Medtronic's most innovative period began a decade ago following an intense set of negotiations with Siemens, our leading competitor in pacemakers, over its violation of Medtronic patents. As a result, Siemens and its successor are paying Medtronic a total of $450 million in royalties over a twelve-year period. In the most important decision we made during my time as CEO, we elected *not* to take the royalties to the bottom line. Instead, we reinvested the royalties in a series of new ventures aimed at intractable disease and launched a series of new ventures as part of a program I called "Reinventing Medtronic."

At the time we were spending over $100 million a year in R&D—about 9 percent of sales—but there was never enough money to fund breakthrough ventures. In reality, all our R&D funds were tied up in existing businesses. We decided to ratchet up Medtronic's R&D spending ratio from 9 percent of revenues to 12 percent, knowing that these investments would not produce any bottom-line return for five to ten years.

Our executive team met to generate creative ideas about what ventures to fund. To get all the ideas on the table, we developed two lists, one of "unmet medical needs" (defined as chronic diseases for which there was no restorative therapy), and the second of potential Medtronic technology applications for implantable medical devices.

Ten years later the new therapies produced by these ventures are offering new life and hope for millions of people suffering from such debilitating diseases as heart failure, Parkinson's disease, cerebral palsy, incontinence, gastrointestinal disease, atrial fibrillation, and epilepsy. As a result of "Reinventing Medtronic," the company has become known for creating miracles for patients suffering from incurable disease. This success is spawning many more creative ideas inside the company to use medical technology to address so-called untreatable diseases.

An Uncommon Miracle That Began with "Failure"

The most important venture turned out to be new therapies for heart failure. The most prevalent disease in the United States, heart failure affects approximately twenty-two million people around the world. It is a progressive disease that leads to the death of more than two million people per year. It is also the most expensive disease, costing $25,000 per patient-year.

From the standpoint of applying Medtronic technology, heart failure was the least obvious disease to pursue. When our venture team talked to heart failure specialists, they were not enthusiastic about using implantable stimulators instead of drugs for treatment. Nevertheless, the venture team began preliminary research on an implantable product and found a group of French physicians eager to pioneer an entirely new therapy for heart failure. The initial trials demonstrated that patients improved measurably after receiving their implants.

When outcomes from human clinical trials were first presented, many physicians called them "a miracle"—patients showed an 80 percent improvement over the best drug therapy, and their quality of life improved remarkably. Formerly bedridden patients were not only up and walking but back to leading more normal lives. Significantly, hospitalization and hospital costs decreased 60 percent.

With such extraordinary clinical results, Medtronic worked with the FDA for an accelerated review. Approval was received in just four months. Since receiving approval, heart failure therapy has become the company's major growth vehicle on its way to becoming a $2 billion business.

Yet Another Miracle: This Time for Parkinson's Disease

Another venture involved the application of deep brain implants to treat Parkinson's disease. It too has become a life-transforming therapy for patients suffering from this terrible disease. The medical genius behind this invention is Dr. Alim Benabid, a pioneering French neurological surgeon. Ten years ago he began to experiment with treating tremor from Parkinson's disease. By implanting an electrode in the brain and connecting it to a Medtronic stimulator, Benabid found he could virtually eliminate the tremors.

Dr. Benabid did not stop with this success. Next he tackled the more advanced symptoms experienced by Parkinson's sufferers: rigidity of the body, immobility, instability in standing, and spastic movements of the arms that make it impossible even to hold a glass. These conditions confine patients to wheelchairs and force them to have continual care just to live from day to day. By placing the electrode deeper in the patient's brain, Benabid found he could virtually eliminate these symptoms, restoring the patient to an active life. The outcomes were so dramatic that Medtronic went full speed ahead with clinical trials. Two years later FDA approval was received, providing the first new therapy for Parkinson's disease in thirty years.

In 1997 Dr. Alim Benabid visited Medtronic headquarters, bringing with him a forty-year-old Belgian patient to meet with Medtronic employees. He described the procedure he had developed and then showed a video of one of his patients before the procedure. The first segment showed a hospital-gowned man who could not stand up, even when held by his nurse. The next segment showed the same man sitting on the floor trying to eat a plate of food with his hands. His motions were so wild and random that his arms and his food were flying all over the room. The tape was so painful to watch that I had to cover my eyes.

Then Benabid shut off the tape. "Michel, please come up here." With that, a handsome young man came out of the audience, bounded up the steps to the stage, and did a pirouette, holding his hands gracefully above his head. Employees gasped as they realized that Michel was the same man shown in the video.

Or was he? As Michel described himself, he was a new man, transformed by his Medtronic neuro-stimulator. He was back at work full time and could do everything he did before he contracted Parkinson's. His depression had gone away, and his old energy had returned. Michel's restoration from this incurable disease to a full, active life is truly a miracle.

Obsoleting Your Business

Medtronic is the world leader in bypass circuits for open-heart surgery. In the mid-1990s Medtronic created a new venture called "minimally invasive cardiac surgery," aimed at revolutionizing the open-heart procedure. This venture faced tremendous resistance from Medtronic's cardiac surgery leadership, which was feeling threatened by an invention that could obsolete its existing business.

For this reason we put the venture under the direction of Vice Chair Glen Nelson, who carefully nurtured it into a going business. The venture team came up with a simple suction system that enables cardiac surgeons to operate on a beating heart. It eliminates the need for the bypass procedure altogether. The "beating heart" procedure is much easier on patients, getting them home sooner and avoiding the memory loss that often results from the bypass procedure. In spite of being criticized by traditional cardiac surgeons, the pioneers who perfected this new surgery turned it into a tremendous success.

Innovation Begets Transformation

These ventures for heart failure, Parkinson's, and "beating heart" surgery all needed nurturing in the early stages when it was unclear where they were headed or whether they would work. We were fortunate to have leaders who were skilled at developing new ventures and were flexible, creative, and patient. Some of the best operating managers exhibit just the opposite characteristics. For this reason new ventures need a protective sponsor until they can stand on their own.

Not all of the new ventures were successful. Some were canceled, others are still developing, and some we just missed out on. The nature of new ventures is that they are very high risk. To succeed, management has to have a high tolerance for failure and not punish the leaders of unsuccessful ventures just because the hoped-for therapy did not materialize. One or two big winners can easily justify a dozen opportunities that do not pan out.

The ventures had a transforming effect on Medtronic. Both internally and externally, their success demonstrated that Medtronic is a company with a heart. The entire organization is now embracing change and innovation as a way of life and as a competitive advantage. These innovations have been a key factor in changing Medtronic's image from the pacemaker company of the 1980s to the innovative, high-growth leader in medical technology for the twenty-first century. More important, the breakthrough innovations resulting from these ventures will restore millions of people to fuller lives in the years ahead and make major contributions to changing the course of some of our most debilitating diseases.

Innovations like these result from employees with a passion to make a difference in the lives of their customers. By appealing to the hearts of employees, leaders can inspire them to creative results that vastly exceed those obtainable by organizations that treat employees as people doing work that just uses their heads and their hands.

Chapter Thirteen

Acquisitions Aren't Just About Money

Acquisitions can be a powerful—and immediate—way to transform, strengthen, and build an enduring organization. Almost overnight, a company can enter new fields or enhance its strategic position in an existing market. When acquired companies are integrated into the existing organization effectively, they can provide organizational stability and a broader range of talent, and rejuvenate the company's culture in the process. Acquisitions can complement organic growth and, in some cases, accelerate it through the addition of new technologies and augmented capabilities.

Therein lies a danger. If leaders rely on acquisitions rather than internal growth for expansion, or to bail themselves out of a jam, eventually they will wind up in trouble. Unlike internal initiatives, the availability and timing of acquisitions cannot be planned or even predicted. No amount of analytical work will ensure the readiness of the right company to join your organization.

As my colleague Glen Nelson was fond of saying, "We just have to be patient until the stars align." For publicly traded companies, that alignment of stars includes the relative stock prices lining up so that a financially viable deal can be done. When the stars do align, the leader must seize the moment and move quickly to get agreement on a transaction.

From the Brink of Disaster to Transformation

Just such an alignment occurred in the fall of 1998, when Medtronic transformed itself by a series of acquisitions costing $9 billion. Looking back on that period, I would like to say that it was all part of a grand plan, well analyzed and well thought out. Nothing could be further from the truth. Making multiple acquisitions in a short period of time rarely works that way.

Ironically, it all began when we were at the lowest point in my ten years as CEO, the spring of 1998, when I was a deeply worried man. Medtronic's growth had declined sharply from the robust levels of previous years. To make matters worse, our executive team was losing confidence in our ability to continue growing and had soured on making acquisitions. I was not sure we could sustain our growth much longer unless we took some bold moves.

This is a difficult situation for the leader of a large organization. At a time like this you have to exude confidence. Everyone watches the leader for signals that the business will be successful and continue growing. On the other hand, as the leader you must be brutally honest with your key executives about the realities of the business so that the leadership team does not kid itself. There is nothing worse than letting false optimism interfere with hard decisions that must be made.

But it was precisely these difficulties that led to the greatest transformation of the company during my tenure as CEO. Just six months later we had announced five major acquisitions and doubled the size of the company. More important, we were able to diversify Medtronic's organization, creating the depth and balance needed to sustain our growth.

Looking back on that period, it is evident that I had good reasons to be concerned about Medtronic's growth prospects. The modest acquisitions made in prior years were not improving revenues as planned. In contrast, our principal competitors, Guidant and Boston Scientific, were still accelerating. Medtronic's pacemaker sales growth had slowed and the defibrillator business, which had been our best growth vehicle, was losing market share to Guidant's new dual-chamber defibrillator.

Medtronic's biggest problem that spring was in angioplasty. In part, our problems stemmed from my worst decision as CEO. Shortly after I was elected, I was approached by the head of an up-

and-coming angioplasty company called Sci-Med about becoming part of Medtronic. We decided against the acquisition because of Sci-Med's legal problems, concerns that angioplasty prices would decline, and a mistaken belief that we could build our fledgling business into a leadership role. This was a huge mistake. Sci-Med resolved its issues and became a market leader, later being acquired by Boston Scientific.

By 1998 our product offerings in angioplasty were still not competitive with the market leaders. Guidant had just introduced a second-generation stent that was stealing the market. Its double-barreled thrust in defibrillators and stents turned Guidant into Medtronic's major competitor. The situation was so grim that I considered dropping out of angioplasty.

The stock market was patiently awaiting our new product offerings and mercifully ignoring our tribulations in angioplasty. Medtronic's stock price was forty times earnings, in spite of our slowing growth rate. We were working hard to meet near-term earnings expectations and not disappoint our shareholders. Our team did yeoman service in keeping earnings up while revenues lagged. That year earnings grew 12 percent on revenue growth of only 7 percent, the smallest increase since I joined the company.

Compounding the problems, several members of Medtronic's executive team opposed further acquisitions because of our inability to make previous acquisitions perform. They felt integration of these acquisitions was taking time, money, and talent away from our core businesses. There were rumblings emanating from Medtronic's pacemaker group that the company should "return to its roots" and pare back exclusively to pacemakers and defibrillators.

In the face of this opposition, I turned to Glen Nelson to see what we could do in the acquisition arena to resolve our growth dilemma. The two of us engaged in an intense set of discussions with potential acquisition candidates. We visited U.S. Surgical, took a hard look at the angioplasty division of Pfizer, and explored the acquisition of Bard's angioplasty business. At one point Glen even considered acquiring all three of them. We concluded that none of these acquisition candidates would solve our growth problem or our angioplasty dilemma.

Moving Ahead

One interesting acquisition candidate was Physio-Control of Redmond, Washington, the market leader in manual defibrillators used in hospitals. It also had established the early lead in the emerging field of automatic external defibrillators (AEDs). We believed the rapid expansion of AEDs to public places, office buildings, airports, and athletic arenas would increase the survival rates for sudden cardiac arrest. Improving survival would not only save thousands of lives but would expand the market for our implantable defibrillators.

In my experience acquisitions often fail, not because of the financials or lack of a strategic rationale, but because of cultural clashes. For a vivid real-time example, look at the current tribulations of DaimlerChrysler. If you can reach agreement first on a common vision, values, and organization structure, the negotiations over money will go a lot faster. For this reason, in my first meeting with the Physio-Control CEO, we talked about our common mission, agreed on our mutual values, discussed the strategy for the combined businesses, and decided how the two cultures would mesh. Price was not mentioned. This approach worked well and led to a rapid agreement in our second meeting.

Nevertheless, I still faced internal opposition. After listening carefully to this opposition, I decided it was time to move forward anyway. We needed make a successful acquisition to regain our confidence, and Physio was that move. Instead of gaining executive committee approval first, I took the decision directly to the Medtronic board. This caused some consternation among the management, but I believed it was preferable to an open split.

The Medtronic board approved the merger for a price of $500 million. When the deal was announced the following day, it was well received by our shareholders and the stock market. Our first deal of 1998 was done. The next month we followed up with the acquisition of a medium-sized cardiac surgery company for $100 million.

That summer I initiated a meeting with the CEO of Sofamor Danek, the world's leading spinal surgery company, based in Memphis. Our analysis of Sofamor was very positive with one major exception: the company had had over four thousand lawsuits filed against it in the infamous pedicle screw cases. *Pedicle screws* are metal objects surgically placed in the back for spinal fusion. They had drawn public attention and subsequent lawsuits several years earlier when a network television show attempted to demonstrate the screws were flawed.

In our first meeting, we proposed a merger of our two companies, talking about the similarities of our cultures and values, and the complementarities of the spinal and neurological surgery businesses. Sofamor's CEO expressed interest in moving forward. Once again, price was never discussed in the initial meeting. Following that meeting, things moved rapidly. The CEO called back to say that his board would agree to the merger if the price was right. I told him that his stock price was so high that Medtronic could not offer a sizable premium, but we would make a fair offer. Two meetings later we had a deal.

We committed to let Sofamor's CEO run the business in an independent manner, provided he could keep revenues and earnings growing at greater than 25 percent per annum. With a handshake on the essentials, we proceeded with due diligence. The deal was valued at $3.7 billion in Medtronic stock, the largest acquisition we had ever made.

Due diligence came down to the question of pedicle screw litigation. To assist us in evaluating the legal risks, our lawyers hired a top tort attorney to assess Sofamor's legal position. Her examination showed that the company had done a brilliant job in mounting defenses against what was proving to be a fraudulent set of cases. These lawsuits had the potential to bankrupt Sofamor Danek, had it not taken the initiative to meet the plaintiffs' attorneys head on. After a thorough discussion of the legal issues with our board, the merger was approved.

The Sofamor Danek acquisition has proven to be the best purchase Medtronic ever made—both financially and in terms of establishing the neurological and spinal business as a major growth vehicle for Medtronic. In the four years since Medtronic acquired Sofamor, its growth in revenues and earnings have exceeded 30 percent per year. This acquisition improved Medtronic's growth rate and helped shift our business profile to more rapidly growing businesses.

Very few companies would have stepped up to the challenge of acquiring Sofamor in the face of the pedicle screw litigation. We saw it as a problem to be managed. Thus far, most of the cases have been thrown out of court, and the remaining cases are in the process of being dismissed. The key lesson here is that you cannot be timid in the face of known business risks. Taking risks that others fear can result in larger returns than anyone believes possible.

Facing the Angioplasty Challenge

Flying home from Sofamor Danek following the merger announcements, I was still worried about our strategic gap in angioplasty. If we abandoned that area altogether, I was concerned that Guidant might wind up with the vast majority of the market, and direct its excess cash back into the pacemaker and defibrillator markets. While we were busy doing our deals, Guidant upped its challenge to Medtronic's pacing business by acquiring the number three manufacturer of pacemakers, more than doubling its share.

I decided we had to make a major move in angioplasty. Even if we never became the leader, we had to blunt Guidant's forays. The best option was to acquire a California high-tech start-up named AVE, which had recently become the leader in the U.S. stent business thanks to an outstanding new product. We met with AVE the following week and, once again, it didn't take long to reach agreement on the fundamentals.

At Medtronic's annual securities analysts' meeting the day following the announcement of the AVE merger, our CFO told the analysts that it would "add ten to twelve cents per share to Medtronic's earnings." However, in the two months that transpired before the deal closed, AVE's competitors aggressively went after its share of the U.S. market. To make matters worse, some security analysts decided that the promised uplift in our earnings was too conservative and that the real number would be more like $0.16–0.18. Expectations for Medtronic's EPS were rising, just as AVE's stent share was falling!

Within two months, it was clear that Medtronic could not make these higher earnings expectations due to declining AVE sales. Much to my chagrin, we held our first and only pre-announcement of an earnings shortfall during my time at Medtronic. Although we were only $0.02 short of expectations, the analysts were furious. Some even accused me of lying to them about AVE's prospects. In spite of the AVE sales decline, we wound up hitting the original $0.10–0.12 uplift in earnings per share that we had predicted for the year. That *still* did not satisfy the analysts.

This was a good lesson for me—albeit an unpleasant one—in just how unmerciful the stock market can be when management disappoints them. Would I do it again, knowing of the risk of an earnings shortfall? You bet! Sometimes it takes this kind of short-term pain to make the strategic transformations needed for the long term.

Weaving the Pieces Together

By the end of January 1999 we had completed five acquisitions at a total cost of $9 billion. These acquisitions doubled the size of Medtronic, increasing revenues from $2.5 billion to $5 billion and our employee base from twelve thousand to twenty-three thousand. Now we had the challenge of integrating these companies into Medtronic and building a broader organization. We wanted to retain key executives, the loyalty and commitment of their employees, and their competitive spirit, all with a minimum of disruption.

To ensure successful integration, we decided on a systematic approach for all five companies that addressed four key issues: leadership of the business, financial leadership, business integration, and cultural integration. COO Art Collins took the lead in the business assimilation and organizational issues, and I led the cultural integration myself.

An integration team was formed for each acquisition, led by a Medtronic executive. Teams included people from the acquired company as well as Medtronic, giving them ownership of the process and responsibility for the outcome. They developed detailed integration plans, complete with timetables and financial impact statements.

I undertook the challenge of imbuing each of our new organizations with the Medtronic mission and values. During the courtship process I had focused on gaining agreement with the CEOs to our mission and shared values. Since each of the three large acquired companies had distinct and well-established cultural norms, getting their employees to understand and embrace Medtronic's mission and values presented a far greater challenge.

Sofamor Danek is a product of its Memphis heritage. Its culture is quite formal; for example, people wear suits and dresses to meetings and are very respectful of the hierarchy, in spite of the CEO's down-to-earth style. AVE is just the opposite. It has a wide-open, free-wheeling California culture where everything seemed to happen spontaneously. People are so informal that it is impossible to tell the managers from the employees. Seattle-based Physio-Control is somewhere in between these two widely disparate cultures. The key point here is that all three cultures are highly successful, and we did not want to disrupt their successful mode of operation.

I felt the Medtronic mission was the perfect vehicle for bringing everyone together. I visited each new location, not just the headquarters. I met with all of our new employees, described Medtronic and its rich heritage, and conducted Mission and Medallion ceremonies. This meant doing twenty mission ceremonies at a dozen locations. During this time I personally presented over eight thousand new employees with their Medtronic medallions.

Going into this process, I had a lot of doubts about how the ceremonies would be received by the new employees; for example, would AVE's California employees find it "too hokey," or would the second-shift machinists in Warsaw, Indiana, find it "too soft"? Quite the contrary. The feedback I got from the employees who attended these sessions was uniformly positive. They were impressed that Medtronic's CEO would meet personally with them in their workplace, and they liked the traditions of the Medtronic culture.

The $9 billion spent on these acquisitions enhanced Medtronic's shareholder value by making us the market leader in key medical technology markets, leading to a $35 billion increase in shareholder value. None of this would have happened had we not had the courage to go against the grain in mid-1998 and take the risks required to transform the company. Nor could it have been done without a strong team at the top, led by Glen Nelson to put the deals together and Art Collins to translate them into operational reality.

We transformed Medtronic forever from the pacemaker company of old, while remaining true to our heritage. In transcending the dark days of early 1998, we earned the right to claim that Medtronic is "the world's leading medical technology company."

Reflections

Many other companies, notably Pfizer, General Electric, Wells Fargo, and Nestlé, have also been successful in building their organizations through a judicious mix of acquisitions and organic growth. The key to success is to avoid becoming dependent on acquisitions for making the numbers. That kind of financial engineering, no matter how cleverly executed, will catch up with you in the end. Instead, acquisitions must be done for strategic reasons, waiting patiently until the right company with the right culture comes along at an acceptable price.

The hidden benefit in strategic acquisitions can be the strengthening of the organization. As the tribulations of AOL Time Warner and DaimlerChrysler illustrate all too well, there is no guarantee that the organizations will work together. The key is the integration process. Acquired companies can bring great creative and technical capabilities with them and challenge the existing organization to sharpen its innovative skills. They can also strengthen the management team with new talent and new approaches to serving customers. As the result of an effective process of integrating acquired companies, companies develop more enduring organizations.

Chapter Fourteen

Shareholders Come Third

Several years ago *Worth Magazine* ran a cover story on Medtronic quoting me as saying, "Shareholders come third." The article went on to describe how Medtronic placed primary emphasis on meeting the needs of its customers and motivating its employees to do so. I expected a negative reaction from Medtronic shareholders to this headline. It never came, perhaps because our shareholders recognized the truth behind it. Companies that put their customers first and empower their employees to serve them will inevitably provide greater growth in shareholder value than those corporations that focus primarily on getting their stock price up and only give lip service to other constituencies.

Meeting the needs and demands of all stakeholders concurrently is a very challenging task, requiring a great deal of skill, patience, and self-discipline. Leaders are continually confronted with the competing interests of their stakeholders. Each group feels that they have a unique claim on you and the ability to influence your decisions. The conflicts among their interests are real and ever-present. Let's look at each of these stakeholder groups and how to address their needs.

Customers

The first purpose of any corporation is to serve its customers. In Medtronic's case, the ultimate customers are patients and the immediate customers are physicians. By teaming with its physician customers to get the best results for their patients, Medtronic serves both groups simultaneously. In making important decisions, Medtronic *always* puts the interests of patients first.

Market share is the best measure of how well a company is serving its customers. Customer satisfaction surveys, market research data, and customer metrics are interesting intermediate measures of customer service, but market share is the bottom line.

Why is market share so important? When your market share is expanding, more leading customers will want to work with you and bring your company their creative ideas and inventions. Increases in share are highly motivating to employees, making the best people want to work for you and giving them the incentive to reach higher levels of performance. Market share gains create higher levels of profitability, enabling larger investments in R&D and market development that sustain future growth.

At Medtronic we tracked market share closely in every business, measuring it quarterly to the nearest one-tenth of a percent. Rather than relying on field reports and market research studies on share trends, we used the published quarterly financial reports of our competitors as the most accurate and reliable source. During the past thirteen years Medtronic's market share has grown dramatically in every business. Consistent market share gains over an extended period of time prove another adage, "When you're growing faster than the market, a lot of good things happen to you." In other words, market share gains create a positively reinforcing cycle.

Employees

Several years ago I was traveling on an airplane and noticed how disagreeable the flight attendants were with the passengers. After the meals were cleared, I asked one attendant who seemed in a particularly bad mood what was going on. Her response was forceful—and memorable. "We are treated so poorly by the management of this airline that we have no motivation to treat passengers well."

The leader's job is to provide an empowering environment that enables employees to serve their customers and provides them the training, education, and support they need. If leaders treat their employees well, employees will treat customers well. It is as simple as that. The front-line employees have the greatest day-to-day influence on customer service, not the management. Look at the difference in service between a Four Seasons hotel and a Sheraton. The leadership of Four Seasons is dedicated to intensive employee training to ensure customers receive the best service.

Medtronic employees are the most empowered and committed to serving customers of any group I know. The Medtronic mission has a very powerful effect in aligning all Medtronic employees with a common purpose, including those in newly acquired organizations. It has been the single most important factor in driving the company's success. This effect was illustrated most vividly in "Global Voices," a seventy-two-question employee survey taken biennially since 1994. Sent to all Medtronic employees around the world, it has a return rate of more than 80 percent, in itself an amazing figure.

When the year 2000 results were compiled, many of us were concerned that the results would decline as Medtronic's workforce had doubled since the previous survey. We were astounded to learn that the four highest-rated questions on the seventy-two-question survey *all related to the mission* and had all improved since the 1998 survey. (See Figure 14.1.) The data was evidence that the mission was getting through to employees, new and old alike, and was a major driver of employee satisfaction. The survey left no doubt that

Figure 14.1 Year 2000 Employee Survey

Top-Rated Questions	Percentage Favorable
1. "My work supports the Medtronic mission."	92%
2. "I really understand Medtronic's mission."	90%
3. "Medtronic's mission is consistent with my values."	84%
4. "I am proud to work for Medtronic."	84%

Note: 18,000 respondents worldwide (80% return).

Medtronic was achieving a high level of alignment between its mission and the personal values of employees.

Shareholders

Meeting the needs of shareholders is an extremely challenging task. To begin with, shareholders comprise many diverse constituencies, each with its own objectives, that rarely if ever speak with a common voice. Which shareholders should you listen to? The long-term shareholder that has held the stock through downturns as well as expansion periods? The speculator who bought the stock recently and wants instant results? The employee shareholders who are depending on their company's stock price for their children's college educations? The retirees who rely on the company's dividends to meet their monthly expenses? Or the short-seller who makes money when the stock goes down and advocates its decline?

Facing this impossible array of conflicting objectives, leaders need to keep their focus on the long-term trend of the stock and not get caught up in day-to-day movements. This is hard to do as your company's investor relations team is continually bombarded with questions from securities analysts and investors about why the stock is going up or down on any given day.

Focus on the Long Term

To keep focus on the long term, the only way to deal with shareholders is to manage them and not let them manage you. It is important to tell your story about your company, rather than just reacting to their questions. Your messages may not always be what they want to hear, but it is more important to get *your* message across. Too many leaders fall prey to the pressures from shareholders and become so reactive that they lose their sense of direction and their ability to make long-term investments. Unfortunately, the market and the media reinforce the notion that the recent trend in a company's stock price is the best measure of how it is doing.

In large measure, the current crisis in the corporate world is the result of CEOs' being overly responsive to pressures exerted by shareholders. Very few have the courage to stand up and say that they will fall short of the analysts' expectations. Their boards have contributed to the problem by pressuring management to meet these expectations. This kind of "short-term-itis" has caused many companies to cut back on the very investments in R&D and market development they need to grow their business and forced them to take shortcuts in accounting entries, hoping the business will improve the following year. But these moves just make next year's mountain higher to climb, and in the end lead to major shortfalls.

Making the Numbers

Having said that, it is important to *make the numbers, every quarter*. It was no coincidence that Medtronic hit the analysts' expectations fifty-five of the last fifty-six quarters. This was not done by financial manipulation or inaccurate accounting. Nor was it done by playing the game so many companies play of setting the bar low enough that it was easy to beat. At Medtronic we did just the opposite: we set the bar high with ambitious targets and then put solid plans in place to reach them. When an analyst commented, "Medtronic made its numbers but had to push hard to do so," my reaction was that we push hard *every quarter* to make the numbers.

Over the last eighteen years Medtronic revenues have grown at 18 percent per year, from $400 million to $7.7 billion. Earnings per share grew even faster, from just $0.04 per share to $1.40 per share, or 22 percent per year. These are exceptional results by any measure, especially for such an extended period. In April 2003, Medtronic reported its seventy-second consecutive quarter of increases in revenues and earnings, dating all the way back to 1985 through three generations of CEOs.

In 1985 Medtronic's market capitalization was only $400 million. By mid-2003 it had grown to $58 billion. Thus Medtronic shareholders saw their share value appreciate at a compound rate of

32 percent per year. In *Fortune* magazine's 2003 survey of 10,000 executives for the "Most Admired" U.S. companies, Medtronic ranked first of 660 companies for "long-term investment value."

Could Medtronic have achieved these increases by focusing primarily on maximizing shareholder value? Absolutely not. It was only because we served patients and our physician customers so well with a wide range of innovations that we saw revenues, profits, and shareholder value increase. We were able to sustain that commitment to customers because of the dedication and passion of employees to the Medtronic mission.

Several times during annual financial reviews a senior executive, feeling the pressure of budget constraints, would recommend that we take a year off from earnings growth so we could reset the bar and not push so hard. This would have been a huge mistake, as we would have lost all the credibility with shareholders we had taken ten years to build.

Transparency

Transparency is key to dealing with shareholders. Communications these days are so fast and open that it is essential for the leadership to communicate exactly the same messages inside and outside the company. Medtronic is completely transparent with shareholders about all events inside the company. To diffuse the false rumors that spread insidiously through Wall Street, securities analysts' meetings and quarterly earnings announcements are open to a wide audience, including the media, and webcast to all shareholders.

Managing Securities Analysts' Expectations

One note of caution: analysts like to give management advice as though they were running the company. It is important to listen to this advice as it provides a valuable independent perspective, but *not* be too responsive to it. Analysts not only have a different perspective from management's, they have different motivations. They can make a recommendation to management, and if it does not work out they just sell the stock. As a leader, you have to live with the consequences of your decisions and still enable your organization to survive and prosper.

As a case in point, we had several suggestions in the early years to spin off the neurological business as unrelated to Medtronic's cardiovascular businesses. We resisted these demands, and neuro has been the company's most rapidly growing business. Institutional shareholders may prefer a company with a singular focus, but that may not be in the company's long-term interest. Because the creation of new growth platforms may take a decade or more, the leader must be patient with these opportunities and not overreact to shareholder pressures. Recently, some analysts expressed mild disappointment that my successor is reinvesting so heavily in R&D instead of letting strong revenues flow to the bottom line. This is in spite of the fact that the company is consistently producing outstanding earnings growth. As he said, that's the price the company has to pay to compete and lead. Fortunately, one securities analyst wisely pointed out, "He's running a business, not a stock."

Even with your best efforts, managing shareholders' expectations can be a challenging task. In early 1996 I was on a two-week family trip in Africa. At the time Medtronic's business was the strongest it had ever been with revenues growing 40 percent and earnings up 50 percent, pushing Medtronic stock to its all-time high. Just as we arrived in Nairobi after eleven days in the bush, the phone rang in our hotel room. Our CFO was on the line. "Bill, the stock is off 25 percent the last three days, because an article in *Barron's* says our growth will slow next year, and the hedge funds are dumping their shares." My immediate reaction was, "Of course, the growth rate will slow. Our target is 15 percent and we've been guiding the market to expect 20 percent. We *never* said we could sustain a 40 percent-50 percent growth rate. So reconfirm our projections, but don't get pressured into higher numbers." Even with spectacular results, we faced a run on the stock we could not control.

Media

Although the media are not usually considered as stakeholders, their influence on corporations is so great that they require a great deal of attention. Many CEOs fear the media or have an antipathy toward them inspired by their power to influence customers and employees. These CEOs try to control the media with carefully placed stories and by putting a proprietary spin on results. Or they avoid interviews and stories out of the fear that their words will be distorted and will look bad. Neither is an effective strategy. The media see through the first approach and simply rely more on securities analysts that have greater credibility. Avoiding the media results in letting someone else tell your story for you, usually securities analysts, competitors, or media personnel.

Along with many high-tech CEOs, I have seen the genuine benefits that an open, forthcoming approach to the media can bring. When you adopt a policy of transparency and telling the same truth inside and outside the company, the media give you the benefit of the doubt and cover your stories. At Medtronic we actively sought publicity for the good things we were doing and the new therapies we were bringing to people with chronic disease. When we had bad news, we broke the full story immediately and were treated fairly by the reporters covering us. This approach gave us exposure and credibility and was far more cost-effective than advertising.

Regulators and Government Officials

The medical technology business is one of the most regulated industries in the world, because of its high product safety risks. In virtually every country, Medtronic has to satisfy both an approval agency and a reimbursement agency, each with its own set of regulations. These agencies have the ability to put your company out of business in their country at any time. They are heavily influenced by their political processes, legal systems, medical communities, and the local media. These issues have to be carefully managed, but they cannot be completely controlled.

Often the interests of these agencies conflict with the desires of physicians and the needs of their patients. There is no simple answer to these conflicts, other than to patiently work through them with the interested parties. Company leadership must be visible and get to know the key officials in each country, as in the end the CEO is held accountable for the actions of the company.

Communities

As corporations become more global, the philosophy of supporting local communities seems to be fading. This is a mistake. First of all, our employees live in these communities, so we have a vested interest in seeing that they offer a high quality of life, good educational opportunities, and a safe environment. If they deteriorate, we not only will be unable to attract the best employees, we will be unable to get current employees to relocate. Too many companies wait until they need something from the community to build relationships rather than doing it consistently over time. Medtronic's philosophy has been to support all communities where we have operations and encourage our employees to volunteer in local service projects.

Stakeholder Reflections

The key to dealing with stakeholder groups is a balanced approach. It rarely serves a leader well to focus on one group to the exclusion of others. All stakeholders have legitimate needs that must be met by the company to the best of its ability. This is the *only* way to achieve exceptional results over the long term.

Of course there are competing interests among stakeholders. The leader's job is to sort them out and see that all stakeholders are well served. For Medtronic the most important stakeholders are the patients. During the past eighteen years Medtronic has restored twenty million people to fuller lives. They are the real miracle of Medtronic's success.

Part Four

Beyond the Bottom Line

The responsibilities of authentic leaders extend well beyond bottom-line success. For an authentic company to succeed for many decades it must have a sound system of governance and build in leadership succession for several generations. At the same time authentic leaders have a role to play in the greater society by tackling public policy issues and addressing challenging societal problems.

Sound governance is an essential element of ensuring the entity is preserved and built for the long term while remaining true to its obligations. Sadly, many leaders have ignored the importance of governance as a way to strengthen the company.

At the end of the day, leaders must pave the way for a successor to lead the company in the next generation while they move on to their next set of challenges.

Chapter Fifteen

Governance Is Governance

In the 1970s Kenneth Dayton, then chairman of Dayton-Hudson (now known as Target), established a remarkable set of governance principles that enabled the company to flourish in spite of takeover attempts, CEO changes, and severe economic downturns. Dayton's principles included a lead director as vice chair of the board, a substantial majority of independent directors, a governance committee, regular executive sessions of the board, extended board meetings to review strategy, evaluation and compensation of its chairman and CEO separately in those roles, term limits for directors, and evaluation of board performance. They were published in a landmark 1984 article in *Harvard Business Review*. Dayton's ideas had a favorable influence on the boards of Minnesota companies like General Mills, 3M, and Medtronic.

Legislating Corporate Governance

If more corporate boards had incorporated Dayton's ideas into their practices, we might have avoided the governance scandals of 2002. Instead, most of these ideas have been adopted in new laws and regulations such as the Sarbanes-Oxley Act, SEC regulations, and NYSE listing standards. These changes will close many loopholes in governance practices.

As a result, every corporate board is taking its "new" responsibilities very seriously and attempting to comply fully with the added regulations. This is necessary, but compliance alone will not prevent future board failures. It is impossible to legislate good governance and board stewardship. What is required is for boards to transform themselves from within, with a dedication to excellent governance. This dedication is fully apparent on the boards on which I have served most recently—Medtronic, Target, Novartis, and Goldman Sachs—and I believe on many other boards.

It is hard to respect the leader of any institution—government, business, or education—that does not practice good governance. Good governance provides the appropriate balance of power for management, but should not in any way compete with or replace management's responsibilities. Governance is governance, not management! If ever there was a need for corporate leaders to advocate and practice sound governance, now is the time. If they don't, our system of capitalism may be at risk.

Unfortunately, in the past far too many CEOs have shown little interest in the balance of power that results from sound governance. As we have witnessed, some of them flagrantly abused the power they had been given. In contrast, authentic leaders know the difference between governance and management, and want the two to be clearly separated so that each can function effectively. They realize strong systems of governance will provide the stability needed when the company faces a crisis.

Boards that acquiesce to powerful CEOs must accept responsibility when the corporation gets into trouble. Yet many boards seem more concerned with hitting analysts' expectations and increasing the stock price than they are with ensuring the company's long-term success.

What Goes on Inside the Boardroom

In serving on numerous corporate boards over the years, I have had the opportunity to participate in a wide range of governance practices. Each board develops its own culture over time, and new board members quickly learn how to fit in with the board's norms. The difference between healthy, productive boards and those that fail to exercise good governance lies in the chemistry between the board and the CEO.

When new CEOs are appointed, they tend to be very responsive and subordinate to their boards as they are establishing their credibility and winning the board's confidence. The independent directors were there long before they were and often are loyal to their predecessors. New CEOs feel in debt to the board that selected them and obliged to conform to board norms.

As time passes, CEOs increasingly take control of their boards, winning the confidence of board members by producing results and presenting their stories in a consistent and compelling manner. CEOs also have greater influence over new board members, because they influence their selection and are usually the one to invite new members to join. So the new members may feel in debt to the CEO instead of the reverse.

All of this is quite normal and not cause for alarm. The deciding factor is how CEOs view their boards and use their relative power. Do they want to control their boards and have them support management's initiatives with a minimum of questions asked? Or do they earnestly seek the advice and counsel of their boards, using them for help in solving difficult problems and as a sounding board for discussion of ideas still in the formative stage?

Some CEOs fall into the trap of treating governance and management as their own personal responsibility. They look at their boards as a necessary evil. CEOs may drive for good bottom-line results while keeping their board members at arm's length regarding how the results are being achieved. As long as the stock price is going up, boards let CEOs control the agenda and passively support them. By the time the results turn sour and the stock goes into free fall, it may be too late. The company may be in the red or headed toward bankruptcy. A former member of the IBM board told me the board was totally shocked in the mid-1990s when IBM turned from one of the world's most profitable companies to an $8 billion loss in less than two years. Had the board not had the courage and wisdom to go outside and recruit Lou Gerstner as CEO, IBM might not exist today as an independent company.

Another example is ABB (ASEA-Brown Boveri). Its former leader Percy Barnevik was revered as one of the top CEOs in Europe for his deal-making abilities and the management processes he established to control ABB's 244 profit centers. The ABB board gave him a free hand in making two hundred acquisitions in just five years, as well as in choosing his successor, Goren Lindahl. When the company went south shortly after Lindahl took over, he was forced to resign. Later Barnevik also resigned as chair. Unbeknownst to the ABB board, Barnevik and Lindahl received one-time pension payments totaling $138 million. Faced with a public outcry when these payments became public, Barnevik and Lindahl voluntarily gave back half of their pensions. Currently, ABB is operating at a loss, bleeding cash, and its $40 billion market has collapsed to $4 billion. A new management team is fighting to turn the company around.

How do boards let this kind of thing happen? Many board members are afraid to challenge a powerful CEO out of fear of being put down, or even fear that the CEO just might quit if they press too hard. Some simply enjoy the prestige and perks of being a director, or at least they did until the recent scandals. Others may have been compromised by receiving additional compensation for their board service in the form of consulting fees or contributions to their favorite organization. All these things can affect the director's objectivity and willingness to challenge the CEO. So boards go along with their CEOs' inappropriate compensation schemes and guaranteed contracts, all of which add to the troubles when the company fails to perform.

A Blueprint for Improved Governance

What's the answer to these problems? Simply stated, we must restore the power of boards of directors to govern corporations. It is the board's responsibility to preserve and build the institution by establishing "a bright line" between the role of governance and management. In so doing, the board provides the oversight to make sure the management is doing its job and acts as an essential check against executives who take excessive risks or cut corners in search of short-term gain. If the board is effective in fulfilling this role, the shareholders will be well served over the long run.

Governance Principles

To achieve clarity over these roles, the independent directors of the board should develop a set of governance principles that delineates the board's responsibilities and provides the procedures for conducting board business. These principles should be published for all shareholders to review. The board should report annually to shareholders on progress against the principles.

In 1995, at the urging of the chair of the nominating committee, the Medtronic board and its corporate secretary developed the Medtronic Principles of Corporate Governance. The new principles were published and distributed to all shareholders at the following year's annual meeting. The nominating committee was renamed the governance committee and, when I assumed additional responsibilities as chairman of the board that year, its chair became the lead director. His advice and guidance were invaluable to me in working collaboratively with the Medtronic board.

Governance Committee

Next the independent directors should establish a governance committee, chaired by an independent director. If a single person holds the positions of board chair and CEO, the chair of this committee becomes the "presiding director" of the board. The governance committee is responsible for nominating new directors for election to the board, assessing the performance of the CEO and of the board, including that of individual directors, and of planning for CEO and management succession. The governance committee chair should also approve the agenda for board meetings to be sure that crucial issues are on the agenda.

Composition of the Board

The governance committee should regularly assess the makeup of the board and the type of new directors needed to assure a diverse set of opinions around the board table. All too often the complacency of the independent directors results in letting CEOs effectively choose new board members as well as their own successors. Term and age limits for director tenure are important to ensure new blood on the board, preferably a term limit of fifteen years and an age limit of seventy.

At a minimum the board must have a majority of independent directors, people with no association with the company as an employee or former owner of a subsidiary. My preference is that two-thirds of the directors be independent. Diversity of directors' experience is essential to ensuring that the CEO gets a broad range of input on important decisions. It is important to have other CEOs on the board, but it is not good to have an all-CEO board as this can lead to too much commonality of thought and reluctance to challenge one another.

Boards should ensure that their new board members attend professional directors' education programs, as well as return every few years for an update on the latest thinking in corporate governance. These programs could ensure a minimum background for all directors in terms of their knowledge of governance.

Medtronic had three CEOs on the board, but we also had four medical doctors, several board members with health care experience, and two technologists. Their diverse opinions, which often conflicted with one another, helped us make sound decisions about new areas of medicine and technology as well as companies to acquire.

Executive Sessions

It is imperative that the governance committee meets regularly in executive session without the CEO present to ensure the candor of its discussions. I find that the discussion becomes much more open and honest when the CEO is not present, and the most important and sensitive issues get raised. Although some CEOs are uncomfortable with these sessions, they are clearly preferable to rump sessions of a few directors at their hotel. In Medtronic's case independent directors meet in executive session three times a year as part of the governance committee. After each meeting, the lead director provides feedback from the session.

Assessing Performance

The independent directors should assess the CEO's performance annually, using a written evaluation form complete with individual comments. After CEOs have reviewed the written feedback, they should have a candid discussion with the board. These sessions can be very constructive and clear up any misunderstandings between the board and CEO.

The self-assessment of the board's performance is straightforward. Many boards use a standard form for each member to comment in writing on the board's overall performance. What's not so easy is the evaluation of individual board members, as board members are reluctant to assess their peers. At Medtronic we gave this responsibility to a small subset of independent directors who were not up for reelection. They assessed the contributions of each board member standing for election and made recommendations to the board as a whole. There have been times when board members were not asked to stand for reelection.

Functioning of the Board

Board meetings themselves must provide adequate time for in-depth discussions of strategies and investments, the risks inherent in them, and the accounting treatments being used. The key to effective board meetings is having open dialogue on new ideas, proposals, and strategies long before they come forward for final approval. As CEO of Medtronic, I found these discussions enormously helpful, as the board kept us from several bad decisions and empowered us to take major risks, such as the $9 billion spent on acquisitions in 1998.

Sometimes it is important to honor the sole director who is prepared to take a stand against the management and the board on an important issue. Several years ago Medtronic was considering the acquisition of a California company that seemed to fit well with our drug delivery business. One board member, who had spent most of his career in pharmaceuticals, felt this acquisition would inevitably pull us into the pharmaceutical business, a field in which we were ill equipped to compete. Although the acquisition gained preliminary approval with an 11–1 vote, I decided a few days later that he was right and, with the board's support, killed the deal.

Board Chemistry

Effective corporate governance requires good chemistry between board members and the CEO. Some tension between the CEO and the board can actually be healthy. It is difficult to build this kind of chemistry if the board meets only six times a year for half a day. For this reason it is useful to take the board on off-site trips to company locations and to have one extended meeting per year lasting two or three days to discuss company strategies in depth.

Chairman and CEO: Two Positions or One?

As a result of the recent failures, many governance experts are calling for American boards to separate the positions of board chair and CEO and not let the same person hold both. Separation is the norm in Europe, as the law or the custom generally requires it, whereas in the U.S. one person usually holds both positions. When teaching governance classes in Europe, I am often challenged by participants about why American boards permit one person to assume both roles.

In my career I have been CEO under a nonexecutive chairman, then chairman and CEO, and finally, chairman with a separate CEO. From my experience I have learned that either the combined role or the split roles can work—or fail. If one person holds both roles, it is essential that the independent directors elect a presiding director. I have seen firsthand just how effective presiding directors can be, in one case in leading the board through an involuntary change in CEOs and in another in empowering the CEO to take on significant challenges.

The key to effective boards lies less in the structure and more in the relationship between the CEO and the leader of the independent directors. If they have a mutual respect and are not struggling for power over each other or the board, governance will flourish. If, however, the CEO dominates the board, then it may fail to exercise proper governance. If the chair or lead director dominates the board, then the CEO may not be able to make timely decisions on behalf of the company.

The Delicate Power Balance

Achieving a balance of power between the board and CEO requires trust, free flow of ideas, and a board that is comfortable challenging even the most powerful CEO. This means straight talk in private sessions with the CEO, so that the board is clear about its expectations. The independent directors should insist that the CEO respect their role and use the board to the fullest.

Attaining this balance does not mean a lessening of the CEO's ability to run the company or respond rapidly to opportunities or crises. In a time of extreme global challenges and intense competition, we need strong CEOs to run our corporations. In fact, clarity over roles can keep the board from overreaching into management's prerogatives and enable the CEO to make decisive decisions.

When It's Time to Change Leaders

One of the hardest things for a board to do is to make changes in leadership in a timely manner. When the company fails to perform, or goes into a state of steady decline after several years of excellent results, the board of directors may be the last to recognize the depth of the problems. By the time it does, it could be too late.

There are several reasons this occurs. Board members are frequently out of touch with the management beneath the CEO and the organization itself so they miss the signals. Or they fail to recognize the company's erosion in market share and competitiveness. Sometimes board members sense that things are not going well but are too polite to confront the CEO while the numbers are good and the stock price is up. Unless they challenge the way the results are being generated, they may not realize that the CEO has sacrificed the company's future or cut corners on accounting and reserves in an effort to hit the market's expectations.

Some CEOs are not candid with their boards out of fear of an overreaction to bad news. Board members have an uneasy feeling but don't have the facts to say, "The emperor has no clothes." A code of silence develops in the boardroom. By the time someone is willing to speak up, the company is in deep trouble. This is why executive sessions among the independent directors, without the CEO or inside directors present, are essential to good governance. Often there is greater unanimity on the board than anyone realizes.

Good News in Governance

Much of the long-standing pattern of weak governance seems to be changing as a result of the recent problems, as boards are taking their responsibilities more seriously. These days the best CEOs want to be recognized for having good governance, almost as much as they want to improve the bottom line. The new requirements for executive sessions are enabling independent directors to discuss the most sensitive issues with and without the CEO and take appropriate action.

For an example of a fully functioning board, let's return to the Target Corporation board, on which I have served since 1993. Target has frequently been cited as having one of the top five boards in the United States. Fifteen years ago the company was confronted by a hostile takeover attempt by Dart Drug, a retailer that never could compare to Target. Thanks to the solidity of the board and its sound governance procedures, the company maintained its independence and went on to create great value for all its stakeholders. Contrast that experience with the Pillsbury Company, which succumbed to a hostile takeover by Grand Metropolitan, in part because the board and management did not have the procedures in place to cope with such an event. Bob Ulrich, Target's current CEO, has combined his brilliant sense of fashion and retail strategy with thoughtful inputs from his board to turn Target into one of the great success stories of the retailing world.

On the other side of the ocean, Dan Vasella of Novartis has worked with his board to become a leader in European governance practices and has used the board's counsel to build a great global company. Well-governed companies like Coca-Cola, Procter & Gamble, Pepsico, General Electric, and Pfizer have provided consistently good returns to their shareholders for decades.

Good governance means good long-term results. It is an essential trait of great companies.

Chapter Sixteen

Sticking Your Neck Out

We deal with lots of criminals in your industry. We have an obligation to seek them out and put them in jail.

   —Dr. David Kessler, FDA Commissioner

Sometimes authentic leaders must go beyond competing in the market to changing public policy. Most business executives, faced with public policy issues that impact their companies, prefer to work these issues behind the scenes, meeting with government officials and their elected representatives to obtain resolution. Politicians and government officials also prefer this kind of face-to-face dialogue, out of the public eye. However, sometimes the behind-the-scenes approach simply does not work, and you are forced to take your issues to the public.

Nokia rewrote the rules for mobile communications when its experts helped establish the Nordic standard, and then lobbied publicly for it to become the European GSM standard. American mobile phone users would be far better off had a powerful American company done the same for the U.S. market. IBM and Microsoft were very vocal in their opposition to being broken up as monopolies, and both are stronger than ever. In contrast, AT&T ultimately capitulated to the government's pressure and wound up a much weaker company.

Medtronic faced a difficult situation in 1992 and 1993 when the breakdown of the FDA approval process made it virtually impossible for American patients to obtain the latest medical technology, which they needed to save their lives. That is why we decided to go public with our concerns about the stagnation of reviews at the FDA. By any measure this was a highly risky strategy, especially given the politically charged environment that existed back then. Had this been an issue solely between the FDA and Medtronic, I seriously doubt we would have taken it to the public. Our real concern was for the many patients who were desperate to gain access to new products.

Unable to get government officials to act on our concerns over patient harm, we decided to make our concerns public, putting us on an irreversible course to get the issues resolved positively. This strategy proved to be highly effective, and patients now have timely access to the latest therapies.

A Crucial Meeting at the FDA

June, 1992: The heads of every major medical device company are sitting in a large conference room, nervously awaiting the arrival of Dr. David Kessler, new commissioner of the FDA. In the eighteen months since Kessler took office, he has refused to meet with the medical device manufacturers, either individually or collectively. Finally, our industry association was able to schedule this meeting, giving us the first opportunity to meet with the man who was making so many waves for our industry.

The meeting is set for 3:00 P.M. At 3:25 the door opens and Commissioner Kessler strides into the room. He delivers a strident speech about his mandate to enforce the law and bring more science to medical devices. Kessler says that time and efficiency in the approval process are *not* the drivers. He speaks darkly of "external forces," probably referring to the attempts of our industry association to put pressure on him with Congress.

Next Kessler asks for questions. At first, no one dares raise his hand. Then a few "softball" questions are offered. Finally, one CEO asks, "Dr. Kessler, everyone in this industry is earnestly attempting to obey the law. But sometimes the FDA laws conflict with other federal laws, and we find ourselves in a situation where we may be in trouble whichever way we go. What do you suggest we do?"

Kessler's response is very direct. "Sir, we deal with lots of criminals in your industry. We have an obligation to seek them out and put them in jail. Next question." If Kessler's intent in that meeting is to get our attention and put the fear of God in us, he is very effective.

The Change Agent at the FDA

David Kessler was appointed by President Bush in late 1990. On paper he was the ideal candidate for the job: medical doctor, lawyer, and staff aide to Senator Edward Kennedy and Senator Orin Hatch. His first major enforcement action came at a food warehouse in Florida when FDA agents impounded Tropicana orange juice and charged Procter & Gamble with labeling the concentrate as "fresh." Kessler was there in person and made national news in his press conference that day. Those of us in the industry found it hard to believe that fresh orange juice was the most pressing problem facing the FDA.

Next Kessler turned his focus to the medical device side of the FDA. He made it clear that he lacked confidence in the scientific rigor and product approval process for our industry. In his first enforcement in our field he shut down the angioplasty division of Bard—the market leader—for failure to report adverse patient events. The CEO of Bard was arrested and escorted in handcuffs from his office. Five years later he was acquitted of criminal charges, but three other executives were convicted.

In early 1992 the breast implant controversy hit the national news. Consumer advocates charged that the manufacturers of silicon breast implants were producing defective products that led to long-term health problems. Dr. Kessler expressed great frustration over the lack of scientific data on breast implants. In the absence of data proving their safety, Kessler ordered silicon breast implants off the market. Plaintiffs' attorneys filed tens of thousands of lawsuits against the manufacturers on behalf of breast implant patients, forcing Dow Corning into bankruptcy and other manufacturers out of business.

This was the setting for us in mid-1992. Representing the largest medical device manufacturer, Medtronic management was especially concerned that we not become a target of the FDA. Our future depended on FDA approval of a number of key new products we had pending before the agency, not just the defibrillator.

In this election year candidate Bill Clinton targeted rising health care costs as his number one issue, aggressively attacking the pharmaceutical industry. He adopted a variation of managed care he labeled "managed competition." Congress was also highly polarized at the time over medical products and the FDA. Congressman John Dingell of Michigan held frequent hearings attacking the FDA for lack of enforcement of the Medical Device Act of 1990. That year Dingell wrote 175 letters to the FDA criticizing its actions.

None of us at Medtronic understood how to reach Dr. Kessler and influence his thinking, so I took on this challenge myself. I believed that if I exposed Medtronic and myself to Kessler, he would come to see Medtronic as a constructive leader in the field, anxious to work with the FDA and committed to doing the right thing for patients.

The Pressure Begins to Build

After the June meeting we mounted an aggressive campaign through every available channel to get Kessler's attention. This included letters from concerned physicians to Kessler, media articles, letters from our industry association, talking to the leaders of the Department of Health and Human Services and making congressional contacts. Senator David Durenberger of Minnesota, the Senate's expert on health care, agreed to take the lead in reaching Kessler, but he too was rebuffed.

An Intervention by Congressman Dingell

Finally, we decided the only way to get Kessler's attention was through his congressional supporters, not just his detractors. So we approached Michigan Congressman John Dingell. This was a high-risk strategy, as Dingell was considered antagonistic to our industry. After the initial meeting with the congressman, we invited his staff to come to Medtronic and meet with us as well as other local medical device companies based in Minnesota.

On the visit of Dingell's staff, I laid it on the line: the actions of the FDA to deny access to high-tech products were causing genuine harm to patients. Two weeks later Congressman Dingell wrote a blazing letter to Kessler, saying, "The Center for Devices appears to be paralyzed." He went on, "Virtually nothing is happening despite the fact that at least some pending approvals offer the only real hope for people in need of lifesaving devices. In this regard, I find the paralysis unconscionable." Dingell praised the medical device companies for their constructive efforts and attacked FDA for the "near anarchy" prevailing in medical devices. The letter sent shock waves through the FDA. Its number one supporter had just turned on the agency.

We continued the public pressure on the FDA at Medtronic's annual shareholders meeting. Vice Chairman Glen Nelson used his time at the podium both to offer a constructive "Medtronic Blueprint for Health Care Reform" and to criticize the FDA's slowness in approving vital products like the Medtronic defibrillator. In interviews after the meeting, I noted that Dr. Kessler had been quoted saying that approval times would double, saying, "Medtronic finds that totally unacceptable." I pointed out that the paralysis at the FDA was forcing patients to go overseas to gain access to the latest medical products, all of which were invented in the United States. Medtronic had also decided to move R&D for our new ventures to Europe, which caused a stir in the press.

The following month the *Washington Post* did a major story on Dingell's letter to Kessler, reprinting it in its entirety and referring to his letters as "Dinglegrams." In the article an unidentified FDA official criticized Dingell. This prompted a second letter to Kessler from Dingell that same day. Dingell bluntly told Kessler "to get with the program" and to "start approving safe devices, while holding unsafe devices off the market."

Tête-à-Têtes with Dr. Kessler

Later that week we had a perfect opportunity to talk to Kessler directly when Senator Durenberger arranged for him to come to Minnesota. We hosted a breakfast event at Medtronic so he could address Medical Alley, the local Minnesota coalition of medical device companies and health care providers.

This gave me an opportunity to describe to Kessler the problem we were facing with the FDA. He expressed real concerns over the attacks on him by our industry association. When I offered to be a moderating influence on this situation, he asked me to meet with him on my next trip to Washington. Just before Thanksgiving, I had the first of three private meetings with Kessler. He was a very different person in his office than at the podium or on television: informal, relaxed, sincere, and open. But he never lost his passion, intensity, or keen political instincts.

In our first meeting Kessler described his frustrations with his medical device center, noting his plans for new leadership. He also was upset with our trade association, accusing it of being antagonistic and of undermining his efforts. I described in some detail the problems the delays were causing patients and physicians. In the end Kessler asked me to take the lead in bringing a more constructive voice to the issues.

The following month Kessler made a major speech on his accomplishments at the FDA. Noting the uproar over medical devices, Kessler said, "You have my word that the FDA is committed to working with the medical device industry so that we can resolve the tough issues." Meanwhile, FDA approval times for medical devices were getting longer and longer. At this point the device center was in such a state of paralysis that Kessler could not fix it in the short term, no matter how hard he tried.

We kept up the public pressure on the FDA with a newspaper editorial I wrote, titled "Patients Are the True Losers If FDA Dawdles." Congressman Dingell also published a long report criticizing the FDA slowdown. At this point the FDA seemed like a deer caught in the headlights, knowing it had to transform itself, yet paralyzed by fear of making mistakes.

FDA Reform: Not a Minute Too Soon

In the November 1994 mid-term elections a dramatic change occurred in Washington. The Republicans, led by Congressman Newt Gingrich, swept into the majority of the House of Representatives, benefiting from a voter backlash against the Clinton health plan. As Speaker of the House, Gingrich began to attack the FDA, saying he would like to "nuke it" and turn everything over to third-party reviewers. At this point approval delays had become outrageous, with the average approval time growing from ten months to twenty-nine months.

In December I gave the keynote address to seven hundred people at the Food & Drug Law Institute annual meeting in Washington. In preparing my talk, I was very nervous about potential retribution from the numerous FDA staffers in the audience. Nevertheless, I decided to be candid and let the chips fall where they might. In the address I described the consequences of continuing delays in FDA approvals on both patients and the industry. I said that the medical industry wanted and needed a strong and competent FDA, but we could not let the current malaise continue to harm patients.

The following year we sensed that the climate was ripe in Congress for genuine FDA reform. Medtronic's new head of government affairs took the lead in preparing the FDA reform legislation, in conjunction with the designated congressional committees. The FDA and plaintiff's attorneys firmly opposed any legislative changes.

Our biggest help in pursuing the legislation came from Minnesota Senator Paul Wellstone, widely known as a consumer advocate. The year before Senator Wellstone had visited Medtronic to meet employees. The meeting started with a recent video of the miraculous response of a Parkinson's patient to Medtronic's new therapy. When the senator got up to speak, he had tears in his eyes as he told our employees how moved he was by the video because both of his parents had died from Parkinson's disease. He clearly understood the patient harm that could result from life-saving products *not* being made available to people that desperately needed them. Tragically, Senator Wellstone and his wife Sheila were killed in an airplane crash in the fall of 2002, just days before he was standing for election to a third term in the U.S. Senate.

Wellstone's support was crucial to rounding up the Democratic votes for the bill and to convincing consumer advocates that reform was in the best interest of patients. One day the Senator called to say that he had had four telephone calls from Ralph Nader, pleading with him to reverse his position, but that he was "hanging tough." Overcoming strong objections from Senator Edward Kennedy, the bill passed the Senate by 98–2 and the House by a voice vote.

In spite of these victories, the battle was not over. In the House-Senate conference committee the FDA and the plaintiff's attorneys joined forces to submarine the bill's most potent passages. On the other side, the medical manufacturers association was taking a very hard line, even on lesser provisions, making it hard for us to negotiate the necessary compromises to get the bill passed and signed in to law.

As chairman of the health industry association, I was eventually able to rally the industry behind the bill. In the end our head of government affairs and I negotiated the final compromises with Senator Kennedy and his staff. The "Food and Drug Administration Modernization Act" passed both houses of Congress in late 1996 and was signed into law. Shortly thereafter, Dr. Kessler resigned as FDA commissioner to become dean of Yale Medical School.

Since the bill's passage, the FDA has made dramatic changes in the review process. Revolutionary new products now routinely get approved in less than the required six months, in sharp contrast to the twenty-nine months it took previously. More important, there have been no major product problems from medical devices like there were in the 1980s.

On June 30, 2001, a seminal event occurred when Vice President Richard Cheney, who has suffered from heart disease for many years, had the Medtronic Gem defibrillator implanted. This event received a great deal of national media coverage and helped the general public understand what a defibrillator is. Three days after receiving the Medtronic defibrillator, the vice president went trout fishing in Wyoming. Asked by a friend if he was tired so soon after his surgery, he said, "The only thing that's tired is my arm from hauling in so many fish!"

At the time, of course, no one suspected the crucial role Mr. Cheney would play in leading our country during and after September 11. Had the FDA approval process not been reformed, it is quite possible that this product would not have been available to help the vice president.

Looking Back on "Going Public"

In retrospect, this story sounds exciting. At the time it was scary. We felt very exposed to retaliatory actions by the FDA staff. Every time we were quoted in the press or published an article, we feared a backlash. Fortunately, it never came. Most companies in this situation would have hidden behind their industry association. That would never have had the impact of getting personally involved and having the courage to speak out publicly against an injustice.

Leadership is about taking risks to see that the right thing gets done. In the end these were the risks required to get the FDA approval process reformed so that desperately sick patients can routinely get the therapies they need to save their lives.

Chapter Seventeen

Preparing for Succession . . . and Moving On

Come, my friends.
'Tis not too late to seek a newer world. . . .
That which we are, we are—
One equal temper of heroic hearts,
Made weak by time and fate, but strong in will
To strive, to seek, to find, and not to yield.
—*Alfred, Lord Tennyson, "Ulysses"*

One of the most important things leaders do is to prepare for their own succession. The mark of authentic leaders is how well their organization does *after* they are gone. It is a source of great pride for me to see my successor take Medtronic to new heights now that I am no longer involved.

What Causes Flawed CEO Selection?

Most board members say their most important responsibility is choosing the CEO. Yet almost as many CEO succession processes fail as succeed. Some boards let their CEOs stay in office well beyond their peak performance. On the other hand, the boards of great companies like Procter & Gamble, Coca-Cola, and General Motors sometimes wind up ousting their new CEOs in less than two years due to flawed processes. In recent years many boards, failing to identify a qualified internal candidate, have been forced to look outside the company for a "star" CEO. Sometimes this works, as it did for IBM, but more often than not it fails, as was the case with Xerox and Maytag.

Many succession problems emanate from the CEO's ambivalence about stepping aside. For people who have dedicated their entire professional lives to becoming CEO, the prospect of giving up this position is not attractive. Having wielded power, it is very difficult to yield it. And when you are healthy and have many years ahead of you, retirement can be a frightening prospect. Questions like "What will I do with all that free time?" "What title will I use?" and "What will happen to my influence?" frequently spring to mind.

The resignation of the chief operating officer is often the signal that there is a problem with the CEO's departure. All too often the CEO and the board suddenly decide the COO just isn't quite good enough to replace the highly experienced CEO. The press release may state that the COO has resigned for personal reasons to pursue other opportunities. Or the COO is recruited away to become CEO of another company.

In this last case the trigger point may be the CEO's reluctance to establish a fixed date for concluding the term. Hence, the heir apparent is forced to choose between waiting around or moving on, not having any idea when or whether the top job will materialize. The COO's departure becomes an excuse for the current CEO to stay on for two to three more years until a new successor can be found.

One of the saddest cases of this phenomenon took place in the 1980s at Abbott Labs, one of the great companies of the pharmaceutical field. During the latter years of the CEO's tenure, three outstanding executives were forced out as being "not quite good enough" to succeed him. All three went on to outstanding careers in the medical field. The last departure caused such a firestorm that the Abbott board replaced the CEO with his CFO.

In *The Hero's Farewell*, Jeffrey Sonnenfeld describes the difficulties departing CEOs have with the loss of "heroic stature" or "heroic mission." Although the stature of being CEO was never that important to me, the sense of mission is. I found myself in Sonnenfeld's profile of the CEO who is "delighted to let their children grow up and live their own lives . . . [and] who know they can re-create their old success in a new situation."

A Succession Failure of My Own

The greatest failure in my career occurred as I was leaving Litton Microwave to join Honeywell. I had groomed an exceptional individual as my successor and thought I had support from corporate management. As soon as I handed in my resignation, I lost all power to influence the decision. Instead of my recommended successor, Litton chose a factory operations expert we had recruited six months earlier. Unsure of himself, he put a hold on all R&D projects and began running the organization like a factory. Eventually, he moved the entire business from Minnesota to Memphis to be closer to his Arkansas farm and two-thirds of the professionals quit. Meanwhile, my candidate resigned and became the highly successful CEO of a major media company. In the end Litton tried to sell the business, failed, and wound up shutting it down. Over time, two thousand people lost their jobs. To this day, I feel responsible for this fiasco.

My Time at the Helm

From the time I joined Medtronic, I was determined not to let this happen again. After being elected CEO, I went to the board with the proposal that I would serve no more than ten years in this capacity. Of course, the board could terminate me at any time for failing to perform; I had no contract, nor did I want one. In setting the ten-year time limit, I felt we could achieve the goals we had set out for my time as CEO. In my experience corporations almost never fare as well after the CEO reaches ten years in office as they do in the first ten years. The exceptions are company founders and Jack Welch, who served twenty years as CEO of GE. The board accepted my proposal on the end date for my term as May 1, 2001.

   The second part of my commitment was that I would have a designated successor agreed upon by the board and ready to take over at least one year prior to that date. The term "designated" did not mean a backup who could become CEO in case of an emergency. Rather, the board would fully agree on the person who would be the next CEO, with only the formality of the vote when we were prepared to make the announcement.

Transition Time

I was committed to ensuring Medtronic would have an outstanding leader as my successor. I wanted to leave the company in the hands of someone with whom I had worked and who believed in the Medtronic mission, values, and vision. I've always believed the CEO's task is not *choosing* a successor (that choice belongs to the board) but *preparing* a successor. The latter takes years of working together, expanded responsibilities, increased delegation, and continuous dialogue. That's why it is so hard to prepare a successor if you have three candidates for the job. Often this sets off a Darwinian struggle and creates a lot of internal politics that are not productive, often leading to the departure of the candidates who are passed over.

It is essential to have the board fully comfortable with the eventual successor, which also takes years of candid discussion, interaction, and close observation. Unless this is done, strong differences may show up at the time of selection; boards often make the wrong choice under the pressure of time. From the first time I met Art Collins, I knew intuitively he was the right person to succeed me. The more I worked with him, the stronger I felt that he should lead Medtronic in the next generation. Fortunately, Medtronic board members felt the same way.

As the end of my tenure grew near, I asked the board for a clear indication that Art was the person to succeed me, to prevent surprises at the time of decision. The lead director and I separately communicated the board's intent directly to Art. This is far better than the approach used by many companies of keeping the leading candidates in the dark. With a clear date in mind, Art was fully prepared to take over in May 2001.

A transition plan was developed over a year in advance. The board asked me to stay as chair for a one-year transition, with Art assuming this additional responsibility in May 2002. The formal vote and announcement were made at the August 2000 shareholders meeting. This led to a seamless transition that enhanced the confidence of our employees, customers, and shareholders that Medtronic would go forward with the same high level of commitment to the Medtronic mission.

. . . And Moving On

The final third of your life is about giving back. Psychologist Erik Erickson calls this the stage of "generativity," the time in our lives when we are in a position to share our wisdom and give back to others. It is also an excellent time to grow without the day-to-day pressures of advancing in your career or making the quarterly numbers.

The key to being fulfilled in the final third of life lies in our desire to continue to grow intellectually and in our hearts. In this regard I have had the benefit of wonderful mentors. The best example is Zyg Nagorski, leader of the Medtronic Seminar on Values and Ethics. Now ninety-one years old and still going strong, Zyg has the intellectual curiosity and the physical stamina to lead a weeklong program where he has to be "on point" the entire time.

In my case, I wanted to move on at a relatively young age so that I would have time to develop my other interests. The key to the personal side of this transition is having something to move *to*, so that you are not just leaving the thing you love. That's why I decided to write this book and become a visiting professor at two exceptional Swiss institutions—IMD, one of Europe's leading business schools, and the Federal Polytechnic (both in Lausanne)—and, more recently, Executive-in-Residence at the Yale School of Management.

Teaching MBAs and corporate executives this past year has been a rewarding experience. I am stimulated by their intellect and their passions for making a difference in the world. Pulling back from the decision-making role at Medtronic has given me the opportunity to reflect on my beliefs and philosophies, to share with others, and to grow intellectually. I am also excited about the many opportunities I have to mentor the leaders of the future and be energized by their hopes and dreams. These mentoring relationships have inspired me about the vast possibilities for the new generation to lead authentically and to make greater contributions to society as a whole. They have broadened my perspectives and enabled me to think more deeply about what is important in life.

In the years ahead I also hope to take part in the debates on important public issues like leadership, corporate governance, and health care. One area of great mutual interest for Penny and me is the George Family Foundation. We created the foundation with gifts of Medtronic stock. Penny serves as president and I am vice president. Our areas of focus are integrative medicine, education, leadership development, and spirituality.

Leadership guru John Kotter challenged me recently as we were discussing some of the things I might do in my next phase, saying, "Bill, you're not thinking nearly big enough. Think back to when you were thirty years old and all the things you have accomplished since then. You've got another thirty years to live. With all the knowledge and wisdom you've acquired in the last thirty years, surely you can accomplish more in the next thirty." Sound advice for all of us.

The Final Day

Let me close with the notes I made on my last day as CEO:

> As I am driving to work, I'm feeling both excited and sad, all rolled up into one. On the surface, I am looking forward to handing the reins over to Art and to moving to the next stage of my life. I'm feeling very good about what we've accomplished in twelve years. The mental checklist of all those we serve feels solid: patients, customers, employees, shareholders, and our communities. I have been getting

positive feedback about their satisfaction with Medtronic and appreciation for the impact we have had on their lives.

Whatever battles we have fought, whatever sacrifices we have made, whatever energy we have expended, it has all been worth it—and more! There is nothing more satisfying in life than a group of people giving their very best toward a common goal and then exceeding it. At this point you want to stop and say, "We did it!" before moving on to the next challenge, but you know the next several challenges are looming in front of you.

Just underneath these very positive feelings is a deep sadness. This is, after all, my last day at Medtronic. The last time to walk in and greet everyone along the way. The last time to stop a marketer, regulator, or engineer to see how his or her project is going. The last day to be settled into that cozy office I have called home for the last twelve years. The last day to work with Bev, my exceptional executive assistant for more than eighteen years.

Deep down, I know I will never pass this way again. I fight back tears, tears of joy and of sadness. The dream I dreamed when I was only a boy has been fulfilled. It was far better than I ever imagined it would be. But now it is time to move on, time to pass the gavel to Art, time to go out into that great world of unknowing. Certainly not time to retire, just to move into the next phase, whatever it may be.

The morning begins with Executive Committee and a report of revenues for FY2001, which ended the previous Friday. We finish early, as the agenda is light. I go back to my office to sort through the files. A steady stream of people knocks on the open door and comes in to say goodbye. Late in the afternoon my long-time assistant Bev comes into my office in tears. She too is leaving and it is very hard for both of us to say goodbye. What greater gift could anyone give than loyalty and total commitment? You cannot ask for it, but you can certainly appreciate it.

Tonight we are combining my going-away event with the dedication of Medtronic's World Headquarters, our new campus, of which I am very proud. At 5:30 P.M. I go down to the main entrance to greet my family. We take pictures in front of new "Rising Person" sculpture (symbol of the Medtronic mission) that stands at the entrance as the guests arrive. Soon it is a mob scene as I can barely say hello to all the people who have come from all over the country to be at this event. Over 450 in all. Everyone is overwhelmed with the beauty of the headquarters, the setting and the general ambiance.

We begin by dedicating the building. Dinner passes all too quickly as Penny and I circulate through the forty-five tables to thank everyone for coming. As dessert is served, it is time for the last act. I get up to make my final speech as CEO.

"If one thing stands out in my twelve years with Medtronic, it is the Medtronic mission. The growth of the company, its spectacular rise in shareholder value, the acquisitions and mergers, the rapid new product development—all of these pale by comparison. The Medtronic mission transcends the everyday struggles, the battles for market share, the vicissitudes of the stock market, the regular changes in the executive ranks. Its light beams on the company's employees like the North Star, providing a constant reference point against which each of us can calibrate our internal compass.

"I did not create the mission. I did not even modify it. The most I can say is that I recognized its power and helped translate it every day to our customers, our employees and our shareholders. In short, I made the Medtronic mission the centerpiece of my years with the company.

"There is a point in time in the career of every Medtronic employee when the mission becomes real to you. Not just a piece of paper or a noble set of words. It becomes real in the form of a human being standing in front of you, restored to a fuller life because of Medtronic and our therapies. That happened to me at my first Holiday Party in 1989, when I met a young man who was eighteen years old and had suffered from cerebral palsy since birth. His name was T.J. Flack. Over the years T.J., his courage and his inspiration have had more influence on my work at Medtronic than any other single person.

"T.J. is now twenty-nine years old. He has graduated from both high school and college. He is employed full time as a financial consultant by PNC bank in Pittsburgh. Before he got the pump T.J. had sixteen surgeries to relieve his spasticity and rigidity. In the past twelve years he has had none. He is on his second pump. The first lasted over ten years. He is on no other medication, just the constant infusion of interthecal baclofen.

"Over the past twelve years Medtronic has restored fifteen million people to fuller lives and renewed health. As powerful as that statistic is, it is not as meaningful as this one life. T.J., as my special guest, please come up and tell your story."

T.J. wheels to the podium, puts on his arm braces, and walks up the three steps to the microphone. He tells the story of his miraculous recovery and his restoration to a full life in a clear, bold voice. As he walks down the stairs, four hundred and fifty people rise as one to give this courageous young man a standing ovation, more heartfelt and more deserving than that given to any CEO. As my son Jeff assists T.J. down the stairs, he says, "T.J., look out there. They are all standing and applauding for you." There are not many dry eyes in the huge conservatory. Even the most analytical among us now understands what Medtronic is all about. No more words are needed.

The rest of the evening passes all too quickly: I introduce Art as my successor, noting that he is the one person who can lead Medtronic to the next level of excellence. In turn, he and Glen announce that the Conservatory of the Medtronic World Headquarters is being dedicated to me and that Governor Jesse Ventura has declared April 30, 2001, as "Bill George Day" in Minnesota. They unveil the magnificent sculpture of "The Healer" by Joe Beeler in front of the new auditorium, seen through the glass screen with the Medtronic mission imprinted on it.

It is over. As Penny and I leave Medtronic for the last time as CEO, one thought remains paramount in my mind: the Medtronic mission and the millions of patients like T.J. for whom Medtronic helped create miracles.

If Not Me, Then Who?
If Not Now, When?

> We shall not cease from exploration,
> And the end of all our exploring,
> Will be to arrive where we started,
> And know the place for the first time.
> —T. S. Eliot, *"Four Quartets"*

In May 1992 my father died in peace at the age of ninety-three and my older son graduated from high school, all in the same week. For me it was the passing of a generation. As a close friend told me, "Bill, you just moved up to the front pew."

It won't be long until you are asked to move to the front pew and take charge—or perhaps you already have been. My advice is, don't wait to be asked. Don't wait until you get the top job.

In thinking about whether to step up and lead, ask yourself these two simple questions:

If not me, then who? If not now, when?

The world needs *your* leadership *today*.

My generation was inspired and motivated by a young president, John F. Kennedy, who said in his inaugural address, "The torch has now been passed to a new generation of Americans." Many responded to his call to serve their country in small ways and large. Just as it was forty years ago, the torch is again being passed to a new generation. To your generation of leaders the trumpet has sounded. If you listen carefully, you will hear the clarion call to lead in a different way than many in my generation have:

To be motivated by your mission, not your money.

To tap into your values, not your ego.

To connect with others through your heart, not your persona.

To live your life with such discipline that you would be proud to read about your behavior on the front page of the *New York Times*.

As a leader, you have the task of engaging the hearts of those you serve and aligning their interests with the interests of the organization you lead. Engaging the hearts of others requires a sense of purpose and an understanding of where you're going. When you find that special alignment, you and your team will have the power to move mountains. Nothing will be able to stand in your way.

What Is Your Unique Calling?

Recently, a young leader complained that his generation seemed to lack any causes to be passionate about. I suggested that he open his eyes and observe the world around him. Seeing the human needs out there doesn't take a magnifying glass. You don't have to look far to see

The pain and suffering caused by poverty, abuse, and discrimination.

The need for healing, in body and in spirit.

The desire for healthy families.

The decline in our environment and our natural resources.

The hunger for security and a sense of well being.

Do any of these challenges strike a resonance deep within you? Can you find your passion and couple it with your ability to make a difference in the world?

Reducing poverty . . .

Eliminating abuse . . .

Stopping discrimination . . .

Helping others heal . . .

Restoring our environment . . .

Building organizations dedicated to service . . .

Feeling safe and secure . . .

Helping people develop themselves . . .

Improving quality of life for others . . .

Bringing joy to the world?

What will be your legacy? At the end of your days, what will you tell your grandchild you did to better humankind? No matter how large or small a difference you make, it will become the legacy that you leave the world.

Consider these challenges society faces as you think about where to devote your passions:

We live in a world of enormous wealth, yet three-quarters of the world's population have barely enough to survive.

With our greater affluence has come increased mental and physical abuse of the helpless and vulnerable.

Forty years after the civil rights movement began, discrimination is still rampant at all levels of our society.

We have the greatest medical technology in history, yet the rate of disease continues to grow.

We abuse our natural resources and ignore the growing contamination of our rivers, our open spaces, our cities, and our environment.

We no longer feel safe or secure in our cities after dark.

We stand idly by as our leaders focus more on serving themselves than their customers.

We merge companies to create ever-larger organizations and then treat the people who made them successful like robots.

We treat quality of life as if it were a distraction from the real work of people.

We ignore the deeper meanings of life and the source of all joy.

As an authentic leader, you *can* change these things. You only need to be your own person, lead in your own style with purpose and passion, be true to your values, build your relationships, practice self-discipline, and lead with your heart.

As much as we want to ensure a happy, secure future for our families and ourselves, we have learned the hard way that money alone is insufficient to provide either security or happiness. But making a difference in the lives of others can bring unlimited joy. Leading a life of significant service can bring unlimited fulfillment. Sharing yourself with others authentically can bring unlimited love.

At the end of the day, what is more important than joy, fulfillment, and love? When we experience them, we will arrive where we started and know the place for the first time.

Medtronic Financial Results

These three charts illustrate the impact of authentic leadership on the company in which the author served as CEO from 1991 through 2001.

Revenue History

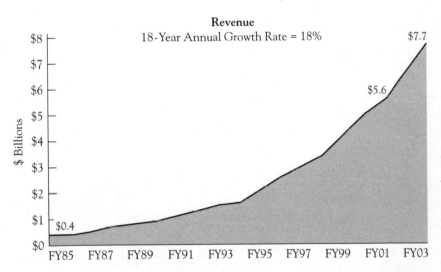

Revenue
18-Year Annual Growth Rate = 18%

Earnings Per Share

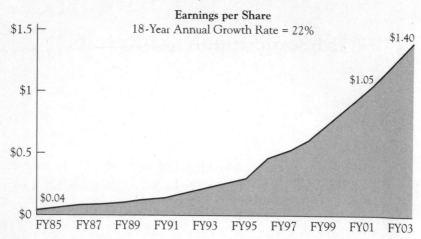

Note: All years restated for poolings.

Market Capitalization

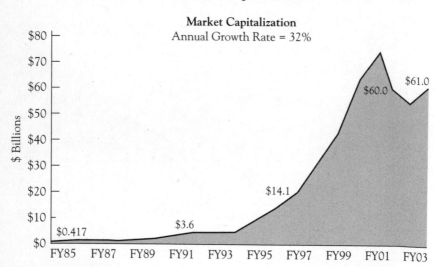

Suggested Reading

Albom, M. *Tuesdays with Morrie*. New York: Doubleday, 1997.

Armstrong, L. *It's Not About the Bike*. New York: Penguin Books, 2002.

Batstone, D. *Saving the Corporate Soul*. San Francisco: Jossey-Bass, 2003.

Bennis, W. *On Becoming a Leader*. Reading, Mass.: Addison-Wesley, 1989.

Bennis, W., and Thomas, R. *Geeks and Geezers*. Boston: Harvard Business School Press, 2002.

Bossidy, L., and Charan, R. *Execution*. New York: Crown Business, 2002.

Buckingham, M., and Coffman, C. *First, Break All the Rules*. New York: Simon & Schuster, 1999.

Carroll, L. *Alice in Wonderland*. New York: Grosset & Dunlap, 1946. (Originally published 1865.)

Cashman, K. *Leadership from the Inside Out*. Provo, Utah: Executive Excellence Publishing, 1998.

Charan, R., and Tichy, N. *Every Business Is a Growth Business*. New York: Random House, 1998.

Christensen, C. *The Innovator's Dilemma*. Boston: Harvard Business School Press, 1997.

Collins, J. *Good to Great*. New York: HarperCollins, 1994.

Collins, J., and Porras, J. *Built to Last*. New York: HarperCollins, 1994.

Covey, S. *The 7 Habits of Highly Effective People*. New York: Simon & Schuster, 1989.

Dalai Lama. *A Simple Path*. London: Thorsons, 2000.

Dante Alighieri. *The Divine Comedy: Inferno, Purgatorio, Paradiso*. (A. Mandelbaum, Trans.). New York: Knopf, 1995.

Dayton, K. "Corporate Governance: The Other Side of the Coin." *Harvard Business Review*, Jan. 1984.

Dell, M. *Direct from Dell*. New York: HarperCollins, 1999.

DePree, M. *Leadership Is an Art*. New York: Doubleday, 1990.

Eliot, T. "Four Quartets." In *The Complete Poem and Plays*. Orlando: Harcourt, Brace, 1935.

Frost, R. "Two Tramps in Mudtime." In *The Poetry of Robert Frost: Collected Poems*. New York: Henry Holt, 1987.

Garten, J. *The Mind of the CEO*. New York: Basic Books, 2001.

Garten, J. *The Politics of Fortune*. Boston: Harvard Business School Press, 2002.

Gergen, D. *Eyewitness to Power*. New York: Simon & Schuster, 2000.

Gerstner, L. *Who Says Elephants Can't Dance*. New York: HarperCollins, 2002.

Gibran, K. *The Prophet*. New York: Knopf, 1951. (Originally published 1923.)

Goethe, J.W.v. *Selected Works*. New York: Knopf, 2000.

Goleman, D. *Emotional Intelligence*. New York: Bantam Books, 1995.

Goleman, D. *Destructive Emotions*. New York: Bantam Books, 2003.

Goleman, D., Boyatzis, R., and McKee, A. *Primal Leadership*. Boston: Harvard Business School Press, 2002.

Greenleaf, R. *Servant Leadership*. Mahwah, N.J.: Paulist Press, 1991. (Originally published 1977.)

Grove, A. *Only the Paranoid Survive*. New York: Currency/Doubleday, 1996.

Jaworski, J. *Synchronicity*. San Francisco: Berrett-Koehler, 1996.

Kotter, J. *Leading Change*. Boston: Harvard Business School Press, 1996.

Kotter, J., and Cohen, D. *The Heart of Change*. Boston: Harvard Business School Press, 2002.

Kouzes, J., and Posner, B. *The Leadership Challenge*. (3rd ed.) San Francisco: Jossey-Bass, 2002.

Krishnamurti, J. *Total Freedom: The Essential Krishnamurti*. San Francisco: Harper San Francisco, 1996.

Krzyzewski, M. *Leading with the Heart*. New York: Warner Books, 2000.

Kushner, H. *When Bad Things Happen to Good People*. New York: G. K. Hall, 1981.

Leaf, C. "Temptation Is All Around Us." *Fortune*, Nov. 18, 2002.

Lorsch, J. *Pawns or Potentates*. Boston: Harvard Business School Press, 1989.

Lorsch, J., and Carter, C. *Back to the Drawing Board*. Boston: Harvard Business School Press, 2003.

Lorsch, J., and Tierney, T. *Aligning the Stars*. Boston: Harvard Business School Press, 2002.

Maccoby, M. *The Productive Narcissist*. Los Angeles: Broadway, 2003.

Mackay, H., and Blanchard, K. *Swim with the Sharks: Without Being Eaten Alive*. New York: Fawcett Books, 1996.

Mandela, N. *Long Walk to Freedom*. Boston: Little, Brown, 1994.

Maslow, A. *Maslow on Management*. New York: Wiley, 1998.

Merck, G. Speech at the Medical College of Virginia at Richmond, Dec. 1, 1950, Merck & Co. Archives.

Moore, G. *Living on the Fault Line*. New York: HarperCollins, 2000.

Mother Theresa. *Meditations from a Simple Path*. New York: Ballantine, 1996.

Neruda, P. *Selected Poems*. (N. Turn, ed.) New York: Penguin Books, 1975.

Oliver, M. *New and Selected Poems*. Boston: Beacon Press, 1992.

Payne, L. *Value Shift*. New York: McGraw-Hill, 2003.

Pfeffer, J. *Managing with Power*. Boston: Harvard Business School Press, 1992.

Remen, R. *Kitchen Table Wisdom*. New York: Riverhead Books, 1996.

Roosevelt, T. "Citizenship in a Republic." In *The Works of Theodore Roosevelt*. New York: Scribner, 1926.

Shakespeare, W. "Julius Caesar." In *The Complete Works of William Shakespeare*. New York: Grammercy Books, 1992.

"The Shareholder Value 100." *Shareholder Value*, Nov./Dec. 2002.

"Shareholders Come Third." *Worth*, Mar. 1999.

Sonnenfeld, J. *The Hero's Farewell*. New York: Oxford University Press, 1988.

Tennyson, A. "Ulysses." In *Selected Poems*. New York: Penguin Books, 1992.

Useem, M. *The Leadership Moment*. New York: Three Rivers Press, 1998.

Walcott, D. "Love After Love." In *Sea Grapes*. New York: Farrar, Straus & Giroux, 1976.

Wellstone, P. *The Conscience of a Liberal*. New York: Random House, 2001.

Whyte, D. *The Heart Aroused*. New York: Currency/Doubleday, 1994.

Acknowledgments

I decided to write this book entirely myself and without the benefit of a ghost writer, but it would not have been possible without the help of my family, friends, and colleagues who assisted me in formulating its ideas and in reviewing the text. I am especially grateful to my wife, Penny, for all her support, patience, and skillful edits throughout the process, as well as my sons, Jeff and Jon, for their ideas and inspiration.

Warren Bennis gave me important guidance and insights in structuring the book, as did my faithful literary agent Jonathon Lazear, who also helped edit the earlier version. Jay Lorsch provided valuable direction early in the process. So did good friends Grace Kahng, Harvey Mackay, Doug Baker, David Lebedoff, and Steve Rothschild. My MBA students at IMD in Switzerland provided the inspiration for many of the ideas in the book, especially Chris Landon who offered insights and skillful editing on numerous occasions. Former Medtronic colleagues Steve Kelmar and Ron Lund also gave me excellent critiques. Along the way I received valuable assistance from Duncan Coombe, Paul Gailey, David Gergen, George Kohlreiser, Bob McCrea, Robert McQueen, Tad Piper, Scott Starr, Howard Stevenson, Andy Van deVen, and David Whyte. Special thanks goes to my loyal assistant, Carol Mierau, for all her efforts.

Working with the superb team at Jossey-Bass, especially editor Susan Williams, has been a delight.

I would like to give special recognition to Earl Bakken and all the employees of Medtronic. Without their passionate dedication to the Medtronic mission, this book would never have been possible.

To all of you, I am deeply grateful.

B.G.

The Author

Bill George was chief executive of Medtronic, the world's leading medical technology company, from 1991 until 2001 and chairman of the board from 1996 to 2002. Currently, he is professor of leadership and governance at IMD in Lausanne, Switzerland, and Executive-in-Residence at Yale University School of Management. He serves on the boards of directors of Goldman Sachs, Novartis, and Target Corporation.

He has been named "Executive of the Year—2001" by the Academy of Management and "Director of the Year—2001–02" by the National Association of Corporate Directors.

He is a board member of American Red Cross, Carnegie Endowment for International Peace, Harvard Business School, and Minneapolis Institute of Arts, and past chair of Allina Health System, Abbott-Northwestern Hospital, United Way of Greater Twin Cities, and Advamed. He and his wife, Penny, created the George Family Foundation.

He has served as an executive with Honeywell and Litton Industries and in the U.S. Department of Defense. He received his BS in industrial engineering from Georgia Tech and MBA from Harvard University, where he was a Baker Scholar.

He is currently focusing on leadership and governance and mentoring next-generation leaders. His articles have been published in *Harvard Business Review*, *Corporate Boards*, *Directors and Boards*, *Corporate Director*, and *Wharton Leadership Digest*.

Index